D1206515

Certified Financial Planner Board of Standards Inc.
owns the certification marks CFP®,
CERTIFIED FINANCIAL PLANNER™ and federally registered
CFP (with flame design) in the U.S.,
which it awards to individuals who successfully
complete CFP Board's initial and ongoing
certification requirements.

50&Forward®
is a registered trademark of
50&Forward, LLC

Devoted to the Journey Ahead®
is a registered trademark of
50&Forward, LLC

All rights reserved. The text of this publication, or any part thereof, may not be reproduced in any manner whatsoever without written permission from the author.

Copyright 2007

ISBN 1-4196-7246-0

To order additional copies of this book please email us at 50andForward@sbcglobal.net or visit www.amazon.com

Printed in the United States of America

Thanks be to God ~
The Giver of Big Dreams

In Loving Memory of
My Dear Friend Neil Beckwith...

I will fondly remember the advice you gave me over 20 years ago while I was studying to become a financial advisor. "One page at a time, Jenna, one page at a time and you will do it." Your simple words of wisdom served me well again as I experienced the peaks and valleys of authoring a book. Thank you for always taking time to listen and believe in me. You taught me not to fear life's challenges, but rather to learn from them and realize I could conquer anything God called me to do. Though your life on earth ended during the writing of this book, your legacy of love, wisdom, and guidance remains.

Dedicated to
My Mother Jean Lane LeValley...

Your unconditional love and support has provided a foundation on which I have been able to follow my dreams. Thank you for intentionally and deliberately choosing to live authentically. In spite of life's obstacles and challenges, you chose to learn from your experiences and pass along valuable life lessons. Through your life, you have demonstrated and taught me the values of healthy living, trusting in God, peace and serenity, forgiveness of self and others, and to use the gifts God blessed me with. During the writing of this book, your constant reminders and reassurance that "everything would work out" were so appreciated. I am honored to call you my best and lifelong friend. I love you!

Special Appreciation to
My Husband, Jim, and
Our Sons – Ryan, Austin & Lane...

I love you more each day. Thank you for your support and patience over the past two and a half years while I was writing (and rewriting!). This book represents the dream and passion God placed in my heart. My hope is that its content will provide a meaningful road map for our family's future. I pray for wisdom as we continue to journey forward together.

Special Thanks to...

My Long-Time Friend Peg Stone
Contributing Writer, Editor & Creative Director

Thank you for helping me pursue my "big dream".
Without your vision, creativity, resourcefulness, and
encouragement this book would not have been a reality.

Kerry Binnington – Artist

Your artistic talent and ability to illustrate our vision on
paper was incredible. You brought pencil drawings to life.
Thank you for your commitment and perseverance.

Carol Knapp – Editor

Thank you for your patience and support during the editing process.
You offered great perspective as a *"50&Forward"* woman.

Lisa Bower – Editor

Your insight was so appreciated.
Thank you for helping get the ball rolling.

RJ Designs – Book Layout

Thank you for being flexible and working with tight deadlines.
Your patience and attention to detail were remarkable.

Ladies...
pack your bags
for

My Life...

My Money...

My Legacy...

The 50&Forward° Journey

A Journey of Possibilities 1

The Planner Perspective 2
~ Devoted to the Journey Ahead
~ The **50&Forward**® Woman
~ Join the Journey: Travel in Style
~ Pursuing My Passion

Now Boarding 10
~ My Money, My Life, My Legacy Itineraries

My Money 17
~ What Matters Most
~ Money Memories
~ Managing My Money: Do I Need Help?
~ Help Wanted: Hiring a Professional Planner
~ Five Powerful P's in a Pod
~ Financial Freedom: Driving the **50&Forward**® Highway

My Life 81
~ Packing Up the Past
~ Living with Forgiving
~ Daring to Dream: a Journey of Possibilities
~ Finding Fulfillment: Living with Passion & Purpose

My Legacy 153
~ Designing a Living, Loving Legacy
~ Creating a Comprehensive Values-Based Estate Plan
  Financial ~ Physical ~ Emotional ~ Spiritual
~ Packing with a Purpose
~ Final Boarding Call.........

"Life is either a daring adventure or nothing at all."

– Helen Keller

A Journey of Possibilities...

I've known Jenna Everett for many years...she is a remarkable woman. It was my privilege to believe in her dream, assisting and encouraging her in creating this important and timely book for women on their *50&Forward®* Journey.

During the countless hours of bringing this project to fruition, we merged aspects of our personalities, talents, passions, hopes, and dreams to create this book. For Jenna, it is her passion to educate and empower women to make wise financial and life choices. For myself, it is my passion to help women discover and write their life story and lessons learned.

As we emersed ourselves in this project, it became clear how God was working out His plan and purpose in our lives, using our unique talents and passions to produce this work...especially in the design of the Comprehensive Values-Based Estate Plan.

Assisting Jenna with writing, editing and creating layout for the book, I experienced many of the same dynamics I hope the readers will encounter as they embrace the power of their dreams. Specifically, believing in and encouraging someone else to follow their dream, you often discover your own possibilities.

We hope your *50&Forward®* Journey of Financial Awareness and Self Discovery helps you realize and believe in the power of your dreams, too! Please record your travel experiences for others to learn from, and by all means, let us know what you discover on your unique journey.

Peg Stone
7/7/07

Planner
Perspective

Devoted to the Journey Ahead...

If you are a woman age 45 to 75 and were told you had ten healthy, productive years to live, how would you answer these questions?

1. What or who would you spend your money on?
2. What dreams would you passionately pursue?
3. What spiritual and emotional legacy would you hope to develop and leave?

The British poet, Robert Browning, wrote *"...the best is yet to be, the last of life, for which the first was made."* If you are a "50&Forward" woman, come along with me.

Society attempts to make us believe we're one purchase away from happiness, but wise women I've worked with over the years value security above any "thing" money can buy. They want to know their financial affairs are in order and well managed, so they can go on to what matters most – the rest of their lives and the legacy they develop and leave for others.

When the end of life on earth is near, surely all of us want to look back on what we've accomplished with a smile and a sense of satisfaction. From this time forward, I invite you to celebrate life and live authentically and deliberately with no regrets or fears. Not yet old, but no longer young, this is a unique time to embrace our journey.

Toward that end, I also invite you to step back in time and examine the path you've journeyed on so far. We all bring to this stage of life a unique set of experiences and accumulated life lessons that contributed to molding us into the women we are today. We can borrow from the insights we've accumulated along the way, but we have only today to plan for and build our futures.

The next phase of your journey is just beginning. The "someday" you've been waiting for – to see the world, write that novel, learn to paint, start an endowment – is here. You've withstood the test of time and now it's *your* time. Come along. Let's pack our bags for the **50&Forward**® journey – there's not a moment to lose!

Jenna Mitchell Everett,
CERTIFIED FINANCIAL PLANNER™
7/7/07

"The future belongs to those who believe in the beauty of their dreams."
– Eleanor Roosevelt

The 50&Forward® Woman

Do you know that women 50 years and older not only comprise the largest segment of the United States population, but are also the healthiest and wealthiest?* While this gives them longevity and potential buying power, I believe it does not address their most important question...

How do I live a meaningful life that allows me to balance my financial, physical, emotional, and spiritual priorities – ultimately leaving a living, loving legacy?

It is common at this stage for women to reflect on their lives and the choices they made. In doing so, many come to realize they have defined success in one or more of the following ways:

~ Homemaking – raising a healthy and happy family
~ Building a career – climbing the corporate ladder
~ Achieving social status – making a name for yourself
~ Accumulating wealth – providing the "quality" of life you desire for yourself and your family
~ Obtaining material possessions – objects that represent "success" and "status" in western culture

When crossing the threshold into their fifties, many women begin to realize the symbols of success they once strived for begin to pale in comparison with, for example, an afternoon helping a child learn to read or volunteering at a homeless shelter. One inspiring author, Bob Buford, refers to this transition as "crossing over from success to significance" in his book *Half Time*.

PrimeTime Women by Marti Barletta, 2007

"Women are much more likely than men to see a realm of unimagined opportunities opening up in the golden years. For most women there are still so many firsts ahead," according to social psychologist Bernice Neugarten.

"An 'ageless person' is someone who is excited and enthused about life," according to Suzy Allegra, author of the book *How to be Ageless*. "They are mindless of their chronological age and aren't swayed by what society says they should be doing. They continue to grow and learn every day...what we gain with age we can't hope to have in our youth."

Now all the wiser, many women are beginning to feel restless, similar to the way they may have felt in young adulthood when the journey lay far ahead and anything and everything seemed possible. However, the big difference is the young women they were then had life's biggest decisions yet to make, and the women they are now have emerged the wiser for all that went wrong as much as for what went right.

"If we could sell our experiences for what they cost us, we would all be millionaires."
— Abigail Van Buren

Join the Journey: Travel in Style

I believe this is an exciting time for many women. It's a time to define your future by exploring your dreams, passions, and purpose. Wherever your journey takes you, the next phase of your life will likely mean creating a balanced lifestyle, focusing on taking better care of yourself, and including in your daily regimen a combination of financial, physical, emotional, and spiritual priorities.

While the **50&Forward**® journey is one you will be sharing with millions, you may feel a bit isolated. Let's face it, juggling careers, relationships, teenagers, aging parents, and households leaves very little time to connect with other fabulous women who are choosing to *"travel in style."* While change is exciting, it can also be a bit scary, leaving you unsure about how to pack for your "own" unique journey. It's like rummaging through your suitcase on a cold winter's day not being able to find your comfy red sweater.

Ladies, it's time to unload the needless baggage that has been weighing you down and begin deliberately planning the rest of your life. Be Brave! Be Bold! Don't let your uncertainty and fear prevent you from moving forward. Today is the day to begin your journey of possibilities!

Pursuing My Passion

I have been a financial planner for nearly 20 years. I am thankful for the privilege of working with such wonderful clients. It is because of them my professional journey continues to be fulfilling and rewarding.

I have listened to and talked with hundreds of people, many of them women, during various stages of the **50&Forward**® journey. While discussing their financial affairs and the importance of planning for the future, I began to notice a clear and consistent pattern of thinking. I began seeing how our life's experiences greatly influence our views and feelings about money. Looking for financial peace of mind, many I've spoken with truly desired to pursue what matters most to them – a secure future for their loved ones and a healthy, productive lifestyle for themselves, one that is balanced financially, physically, emotionally, and spiritually.

The concerns and life experiences of many amazing women (and incredible men!) were the inspiration for writing this book. I am grateful to them for allowing me to share their stories. Although I have changed their names, perhaps you will recognize a commonality between their experiences and your own. My hope is that their stories will educate and empower you with wise financial and life principles, aimed at protecting and balancing your financial, physical, emotional, and spiritual well-being.

I am first and foremost a professional when it comes to giving financial advice, but as a woman I am in tune with other women's thoughts, emotions, and concerns. As you begin your journey forward, I would be honored if you would think of me as your tour guide and consider this book as a personal road map to help you navigate your own authentic *50&Forward®* journey.

I am devoted to the journey ahead, and it is my passion to help inspire and equip you for the unique voyage that awaits. I encourage you to pack only the necessities...and experience how free you'll feel traveling light! Let go of the ordinary and embrace the extraordinary.

Oh, one last thing...feel free to record your travels on the "Points to Ponder" pages of the "My Money," "My Life," and "My Legacy" sections of this book so others can experience and learn from your life's journey. Younger generations will be looking for new role models!

Ladies...pack your bags! You're in for the journey of a lifetime!

Now Boarding

My Money…

My Life…

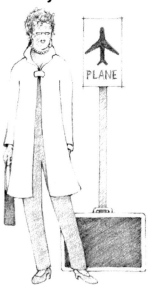

My Legacy…

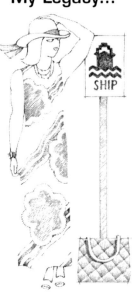

My Money...

If you are like most women, the fear of running out of money may keep you from embarking on the breathtaking *50&Forward®* journey. A common question asked by clients sounds something like, "How do I know what to pack in my bags if I'm not even sure I can afford to take the trip?"

This leg of your journey will give you an opportunity to consider just what money means to you. I want to help you understand how your past experiences and the old lessons you've learned about money can influence the way you earn, save, spend, and invest, both now and in the future. It's important to evaluate your future needs and goals and what it costs to achieve them. My goal is to get you where you want to go!

Before determining where you would like your journey to take you, it's beneficial to plan ahead by preparing a simple financial "to do" list that will help you examine what is most important to you. Knowing how to manage your goals will impact both your financial security and financial peace of mind.

For those of you who are new to organizing and coordinating your financial affairs, I'll share insights on the importance of finding, interviewing, and hiring professionals best suited to help you. Bankers, brokers, financial advisors, insurance agents, financial planners, and investment advisors may all have sound advice when it comes to managing your money, but there is no "one size fits all." I will help you choose the right financial professional who understands **your** journey; otherwise, the whole process can leave you more confused, disheartened, and disillusioned then ever!

We'll take a special "side trip" to examine the many financial planning options available to you. Again, no "one size fits all." For example, you may say that your goal is to be financially secure when you retire, but what exactly does that mean to you? Beyond being able to pay your bills, are there more satisfying outcomes to being financially secure? What emotional and spiritual needs do you hope will be met and what dreams fulfilled?

You will also be introduced to several women traveling the *50&Forward*® journey through their "travel logs." I hope their stories will provide you with insights and inspiration for managing your own financial affairs. Additionally, I will provide you with suggested best practices I have shared with these women in what I refer to as "advisor travel tips."

The exciting *50&Forward*® journey is about your quality of life. By taking control, organizing your finances, and tying up loose ends, you'll find yourself empowered, equipped, and free to move on. Peace of mind and assurance will be your traveling companions, allowing you to engage in the most adventurous stage of life yet to come. All the while, you'll be discovering and living your dreams, finding meaning in the journey, and developing your living legacy.

My Life...

The **50&Forward**® journey is about honoring your life. After all, you've spent 50 or more years of your life piecing together different experiences to arrive at this place in your journey. As you prepare for the exciting road ahead, I encourage you to pack lightly and take only the necessities. I believe less is more and simplicity is the key to living deliberately and intentionally.

In this section, I have made arrangements for you to examine your journey up to this point. Since I know you may have experienced some turbulence along the way, I've taken the liberty of renting you a smooth-performance 1964 Mustang convertible. I want you to experience the open road and the breathtaking scenery whizzing by as you put the top down and let your hair blow freely in the breeze. Instead of moving forward, you will be traveling down the familiar roads of your past.

Open your heart and mind as you embrace your previous experiences and reminisce. I invite you to begin acknowledging the important connection between the memories of your past and their influence on both the present and the future.

For your convenience, I have provided you with "travel logs" introducing you to women who were intentional and deliberate about the choices they made to pursue a life of fulfillment. Additionally, you will be provided with travel exercises called "side trips" allowing you to log your thoughts and examine the most important life lessons you've learned along the way.

As you begin to pack your bags for your **50&Forward**® journey, I highly recommend tossing out negative thoughts, fears, and old grievances. This will help lighten your load. In their place, find room for a positive attitude, forgiveness (of yourself and others), passion, purpose, and your fondest dreams.

My Legacy...

The **50&Forward**® journey is also about embracing the future, living authentically – with passion and purpose – and designing a living, loving legacy.

Most women would agree you can't disregard your past or the legacy that was handed down to you, nor will your children, grandchildren, great-grandchildren, or other loved ones disregard theirs. All of us are products of our pasts, the environment we grew up in, and the experiences and situations to which we've been exposed, both positive and negative. By acknowledging how these choices impacted our lives financially, physically, emotionally, and spiritually, we will be better prepared to design and leave our own unique legacy.

All of us will leave a legacy, good or bad, planned or unplanned, and we will pass something down to future generations. A decision to do *nothing* is also a choice and unfortunately it can become the legacy we pass down. Don't leave this important truth to chance.

On this leg of your journey, I invite you to reflect on your life's purpose. As we grow older, most of us also grow in wisdom. We tend to focus more on relationships and personal values and less on money, image, and material possessions.

Moreover, gone are the days of the simple estate plan. I will introduce you to a unique version of what I refer to as a "comprehensive values-based estate plan" – a plan that includes not only traditional estate planning documents, but also values-based statements expressing your own unique financial, physical, emotional, and spiritual thoughts, viewpoints, and desires.

I will also share with you the importance of writing your life story. Remember, everyone has a story to share. If you don't tell yours – who will? Your loved ones will better understand you if they know how you arrived at this point in your journey. Perhaps it's time to be intentional about taking the time to share your life's adventure with those you love. Just think of your life story as a gift – a wonderful, easy to read, authentic road map!

My Money

18 ——————— My Money

What Matters Most

As you assess your own financial circumstances and attitudes toward aging, how do you fare compared to your fellow travelers along the *50&Forward*® highway? If you haven't adequately prepared for the years ahead, you may be feeling more or less overwhelmed. Please know you are not alone!

Whether you are a novice or an experienced traveler on the *50&Forward*® journey, I believe it will be helpful to take a look at what money means to you and how handling it makes you feel. Ultimately, I'd like to help you understand how your past experiences with money and lessons learned, good or bad, have influenced your emotional response to how your money is earned, saved, spent, and invested.

The adage "money can't buy happiness" may be true, but the lack of money can lead to certain unhappiness if you are prevented from living worry-free. Money is merely a medium of exchange which, in sufficient amounts, wisely handled, provides the financial freedom that enables us to remain independent. Money buys opportunity and the freedom to make choices. Without it, or without sufficient amounts of it, your destiny will be decided for you rather than by you.

Money is not the root of all evil. That's a popular misquote of the phrase attributed to the Apostle Paul in the New Testament of the Bible. What Paul actually said was, *"For the love of money is the root of all evil."* 1 Timothy 6:10.

It's logical that people without money spend much more time and energy thinking about it than those who have money and are financially secure. That being said, those who have weathered life's ups and downs, arriving at midlife wiser and more respectful of what money can and can't buy, often realize that the pursuit of riches alone is a very shallow way of living.

Failure to plan one's financial affairs causes many people to spin their wheels when they ought to be rolling along pursuing the rest of their lives, excited, not worried, about what may be waiting around the next bend in the road.

At times, for example, the decision to work or not work is predicated on income, since many people approaching retirement find they haven't saved enough money for a comfortable future. Others make the choice to keep working because they enjoy their work and desire to remain productive and engaged in society. Whenever you choose to retire, it will take money to live another 30 years or more.

If you're feeling "stuck" behind the wheel, it's time to take control. Organize your itinerary and tie up loose ends so you feel empowered to move ahead with peace of mind and assurance that your financial affairs, including the legacy you want to leave your loved ones, are in order.

Whether you are just beginning your *50&Forward* journey or a seasoned traveler on the *50&Forward* highway, wise financial planning can make all the difference between choosing to work and needing to work. Whether you are in the first or second category often depends on finding the right financial advisor, a knowledgeable professional, who really listens and can help you realize your dreams for the future.

I know many of you worry about not having enough money to experience life's breathtaking journey of possibilities. In talking with so many women, I have learned they are unsure about how their future financial security will be impacted by their present spending and investment choices.

Ladies, help is on the way!

Money Memories...

As I mentioned earlier, I am convinced the beliefs each of us hold about money are formed at an early age, either consciously or unconsciously. Additionally, I believe the feelings we have about money and its purpose in our lives comes from what we experienced during our youths.

If you were born before 1946, you grew up in the so-called "silent generation," when times were particularly hard as a result of the stock market crash in 1929 and the depression era that followed. The financial setback Americans and much of the world faced during the 1930s was made worse by the loss of manpower during WWII and subsequent rationing for the war effort.

If you grew up in a typical household during that difficult era between 1929 and 1945, you most likely saw your family stash whatever money they could save in secret hideaways. Mistrust in banks prevailed at that time (as seen in one of my favorite movies *It's a Wonderful Life*), and for good reason, considering how many banks failed in the fallout from the stock market crash. We've heard stories from our clients about watching their parents hide $1, $5, and $10 bills in ice or frozen fish; in cans, jars, and metal boxes buried underground; in envelopes taped to the backs of dressers, or stuffed in mattresses and luggage.

I've observed that the lessons learned by people who grew up in the "silent generation" about earning, saving, investing, and spending money include:

~ Jobs are hard to find and money is in short supply
~ Life is full of peril, so be prepared
~ Hiding money brings security and peace of mind
~ Buy only what you need
~ Respect the value of a hard-earned dollar and never take it for granted

After the war, men returning home took advantage of the GI (Government Issue) bill to train for high-paying careers in a booming post-war economy. They enrolled in college, got married, and started families of their own. Consequently, their children, the "baby boomer" generation, born between 1946 and 1964, inherited from their parents' sacrifices and hard work all the advantages of a relatively affluent society.

Growing up less fearful than their parents, I've also observed that the "boomers" have adopted very different attitudes about earning, saving, investing, and spending money. Lessons and perceptions they picked up include:

~ Opportunities are plentiful
~ Money is abundant
~ America is a super power and will continue to be
~ If I don't have the cash for something I want or need, I'll borrow it
~ If I don't like my current job, I'll just go find another one

With the onset of credit card use in the late 1970s, the concept of savings went by the wayside. "Buy now and pay later" became a major theme of the baby boomer set.

My Money...
Side Trip
#1

What Matters Most?

Whether you are a part of the "silent generation" or the "baby boomer" generation, today is the day to evaluate what money means to you and how you want to spend it. Your lifestyle choices will impact the quality of your life for the rest of your life. At stake are your dreams and goals as well as the legacy you develop and leave for others.

Side Trip #1 Directions

1. In this exercise you'll make a list of anything you want to spend money on – practical, essential or frivolous.

2. Place an "x" in appropriate columns as shown in the example.

3. Evaluate your responses. This is the beginning of your journey of financial awareness and self discovery.

Example

Financial "To Do" List

Financial "To Do" List	Brings instant gratification	Provides lasting fulfillment	Brings peace of mind	One of my dreams	I'm passionate about this	Brings purpose/meaning	Part of my lasting legacy	TOTAL	Priorities – greatest to least
Buy hot red sports car	X			X				2	4
Pay college tuition for self or family member		X	X	X			X	4	2
Spend money for cosmetic surgery	X		X	X				3	3
Paying off debt	X	X	X	X		X	X	6	1
Buy a vacation and/or second home									
Finance exotic travel									

Start your own list here...

Financial "To Do" List Place your name here	Brings instant gratification	Provides lasting fulfillment	Brings peace of mind	One of my dreams	I'm passionate about this	Brings purpose/meaning	Part of my lasting legacy	TOTAL	Priorities – greatest to least

Now for the moment of truth!

Total the number of "x"s in each row (see example on page 26). Examine your totals for each item on your financial "to do" list. Rank them in order of greatest to least in the left hand "priorities" column. *The higher the number, the greater the emotional return on your financial investment.*

~ Advisor Travel Tip: ~

During my tenure as a CFP® professional, I have seen a pattern among clients leading me to believe that women on the *50&Forward* journey who understand the importance of making "values-based" financial choices are those who typically achieve financial peace of mind. These are the women who know what is truly significant and meaningful. They choose to live authentically, embrace their dreams, pursue their passions, and are deliberate and intentional about developing and leaving a living, loving legacy.

Ladies, this is the beginning of understanding the importance of values-based financial and life planning.

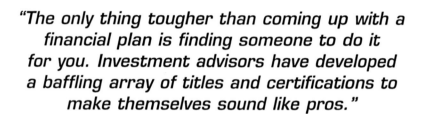

"The only thing tougher than coming up with a financial plan is finding someone to do it for you. Investment advisors have developed a baffling array of titles and certifications to make themselves sound like pros."

– Wall Street Journal, January 29, 2006

Managing My Money: Do I Need Help?

For those of you pondering the benefits of interviewing and hiring a financial professional, you will find this section very helpful.

In the last chapter, I asked you to list your financial "to dos"; what you'd like to spend money on and determine what is most important to you. While your list may be shorter or longer depending on your values and/or circumstances, if you're like most people, you may be wondering how you can maintain your current standard of living, take your dream vacation, buy a hot red sports car, have cosmetic surgery, redecorate or buy a second home, spoil your grandchildren, finance a college education, fund potential health care needs, give back to your favorite charity *and* leave a lasting legacy.

Are you confused and overwhelmed thinking about *all* your goals and dreams and how to prioritize and attain them? If you have tried to do your own financial planning, you know what a time consuming and daunting task it can be. It's a full-time job just keeping up with the markets, interest rates, tax laws, and constantly changing rules and regulations surrounding the financial industry. Tracking your financial plans, goals, and progress can be quite time consuming as well.

It's my unwavering belief that, given the complexities of today's financial world, most consumers simply are not equipped with the expertise to manage their own financial affairs without professional guidance.

Let's consider, for example, the investment arena.

During 2007, our national economy has experienced stress in both the bond and credit markets due to the housing recession. This has significantly impacted low grade bond prices and has also effected government, intermediate and corporate bond prices. Moreover, variances in the performance of domestic, international, growth, and value stocks, and the use of sector specific holdings like oil, energy, timber, real estate, and health care- both domestic and abroad- have nearly overwhelmed many consumers. The constantly changing investment arena can easily cause confusion, fear, and even paralysis regarding making the "right" choices.

It's been insightful that even during a relatively low inflationary and income tax environment and good market conditions (particularly during 2006) many consumers did not experience much growth in their financial assets simply because they were unsure and fearful about where to invest their money.

Perhaps you have tried to manage your financial affairs on your own and found that the "jargon" alone can be very bewildering. Or perhaps you have sought the help of a financial professional only to be left disillusioned by the integrity of the process or individual.

Others of you may have worked with professionals who left you feeling intimidated or uneasy by their use of financial lingo (and perhaps a bit of ego!) – pondering the meaning of key financial terms that come second nature to most financial professionals. Terms including low grade, core holdings, sector specific, ETF's, tax efficiency, Russell 1000, efficient frontier, estate tax reduction, S&P500, standard deviation, PE ratio, inverted yield curve, tax control triangle, mutual funds, asset classes, mid-cap stocks, small-cap stocks, growth vs. value, etc. can leave you feeling paralyzed! Phew! Raise your hand if you find that mumbo-jumbo overwhelming. Many people feel just like you!

My recommendation? Find a seasoned financial professional who won't leave you feeling foolish or, worse yet, take advantage of you by talking over your head. If chosen wisely, he or she can provide the knowledgeable advice you've been looking for and the best opportunity for moving forward.

Over the years, my husband, Jim, (also a CERTIFIED FINANCIAL PLANNER™ practitioner) and I have learned the importance of talking in language clients can understand. We've also learned that one of our key roles is to help clients make prudent, strategic decisions based on a disciplined approach. We attempt to take as much emotion out of the investment planning process as possible by helping clients draft an Investment Policy Statement prior to implementing an investment portfolio.

An Investment Policy Statement (IPS) documents your annual return target. In other words, the return you would like to achieve and the level of risk and volatility you are willing to accept. The IPS also establishes target investment allocations. In other words, based on history, what percentage of your money you may want to consider having in various investment categories (stocks, bonds, cash, real estate, internationals, etc.) given the level of risk and volatility you are comfortable with.

This exercise enables your financial professional to merge "science" (historical data) with "art" (opportunities based on current economic conditions and your unique goals). This approach helps financial professionals rebalance their clients' portfolios based on specific agreed upon goals and brings discipline and informed decision making to the investment planning process.

In my estimation, this is one of the greatest benefits of having a professional advisor working with you – someone who takes a disciplined, objective approach to financial and investment planning. The financial markets will continue to be volatile. Our job is to help clients navigate through that volatility. Too many people allow normal variations in the financial markets to impact their day-to-day emotions and decisions. In turn, this causes people to make ill-fated emotional decisions.

A disciplined, tenured financial professional can give you valuable guidance for your journey forward, guidance that takes into account your personal goals, dreams, and financial dynamics.

My
Money...

Side Trip
#2

To Hire or Not to Hire - Do I Need a Professional?

Side Trip #2 Directions...

Here are some of the most common questions asked by people like you who are considering whether or not to hire a financial professional. Take a look at the following questions and see how many you can answer with confidence.

~ Will I have enough money to last as long as I do?

~ What if I retire early? Will I need a part-time job to support my lifestyle?

~ How do I determine my net worth?

~ Should I plan on taking equity out of my home, either through a reverse mortgage or a step down in size, location and/or quality?

~ How will a career change impact my financial future?

~ Can I afford to fund the items on my financial to do list? See page 27.

~ How will the financial markets affect my portfolio?

~ What impact will inflation have on my financial plans?

~ How much risk am I taking and how do I measure it?

~ How much risk should I take?

~ What is my biggest potential roadblock?

~ Will I be able to maintain my monthly income needs?

~ What can I expect from Social Security?

~ What if I require long-term care assistance or have an extended illness?

~ How much life insurance do I need?

~ Am I adequately insured in case of disability?

~ How can I lower my income taxes?

~ Should I consider a Roth IRA?

~ What is tax diversification?

~ How do I know I have all the appropriate estate planning documents given my goals?

~ What should I do with my retirement plans including pension and 401K?

~ Can I afford to give away money to my family or favorite charity now?

Confused? Overwhelmed? If you aren't certain about how to answer any or all of these questions, it may be time to consider hiring a quality financial professional to work with you on your *50&Forward* journey.

~ Advisor Travel Tip: ~

One thing I know for sure: many women who live with dreams, passion, and purpose know how important it is to chart a course of action and find the necessary resources to help them reach their goals. They recognize the value of hiring a reputable financial professional.

Pamela, 61
Widow Designing a Values-Based Estate Plan

Pamela, a petite powerhouse with a short salt and pepper pixie haircut, came to our office directly from yoga – an exercise and stretching class she considered a "must have" in order to feel physically and mentally alive. Her attorney had advised her to come to us for professional advice.

Twice a widow with children from each marriage, Pamela expressed she wanted to be prudent, but beyond that had no interest in managing her own finances.

"I want to be fair to my children, but I also want to teach them the value of charitable giving. It's important to me to leave a legacy for my family and for my community. I know that means making wise investments, but it all seems so overwhelming," she said.

Pamela also wanted to make sure her own future was secure so she could continue participating in yoga and other activities that would keep her active, happy, and healthy.

What Pamela needed was a plan. Together we began to "brainstorm" until we found the strategy that was right for her particular circumstances. The more she talked about her personal life and what was most important to her, the better equipped I became to help her plan for her goals, both financially and emotionally.

Because I recognized how overwhelmed Pamela appeared to be, I took the time to listen carefully to her story so I could adequately address her needs and concerns. After establishing a rapport with her, we reviewed her entire investment portfolio and current estate plans. In an effort to meet her needs, our first steps included designing a conservative investment portfolio and discussing the strategy of using specific trusts to meet her estate planning goals. The objective was to meet Pamela's income needs while at the same time incorporating income tax and estate tax advantages. Our next step was to set up a series of meetings with her attorney to design a comprehensive estate plan.

~ Advisor Travel Tip: ~

A good advisor will listen objectively and assist you in designing a customized plan to meet your unique needs and goals while also addressing personal income potential and estate tax advantages.

Travel Log

John, 62, Mary, 59
Planning for Retirement

John, wearing a crisp, white, button-down shirt and black "cheater" glasses perched halfway down his nose, crossed his legs and said, "Jenna, we're excited about retirement and have been saving for this day for many years."

John's wife, Mary, leaning toward me and away from John with a slightly worried expression on her face added, "We're excited about the future, but at the same time I have to admit I have butterflies in my stomach. We have so many questions."

It was clear that although Mary had always trusted John to take care of their finances, she needed assurance from a professional third party that they were indeed moving in the right direction. She and John had spent the last several years anticipating and visualizing their retirement dreams which included spending more time with their nine grandchildren, traveling the globe, and volunteering time to their favorite organization.

Both wondered what to do with their company 401K rollovers, how to make their money work hard for them, and how taxes and inflation could impact their long-term goals. In addition, they had questions regarding health insurance, long-term care, and estate planning.

They came to me for a comprehensive look at their financial situation, and together we went to work drawing up a dynamic financial plan that addressed their needs and concerns regarding cash flow projections, portfolio design, 401K rollover ideas, tax reduction techniques, and protection planning (health insurance and long-term care). Additionally, we discussed comprehensive values-based estate planning with their attorney.

~ Advisor Travel Tip: ~

We have many well-educated clients who understand the dynamics of financial and investment planning. These clients realize the value of hiring a financial professional to objectively affirm good choices and offer other options that may be in their best interest. We know from our clients' feedback that working with a quality professional can provide a feeling of security and therefore make the journey more enjoyable.

Travel Log

Charles, 56, Sharon, 50
Husband's Job Outsourced

Appearing as nervous as they might be on the 18th hole with a one stroke lead over their competition, avid golfers Charles and Sharon looked a bit frazzled as they took their seats in my office. Charles bobbed his head up and down as we talked and Sharon clasped and unclasped her hands in her lap.

"We reached our goal of having Sharon stay home until our two sons were raised, and now with both of them in college, we were feeling quite good about our retirement," Charles said, adding, "until all of a sudden, with little warning, I learned my job was going to be outsourced. Now I'm not sure where we stand."

Unfortunately, Charles and Sharon's situation is becoming increasingly common. After discussing their concerns, goals, and vision for the future, I spent several hours evaluating where the two of them stood in relation to their goals and prepared a financial plan tailored to meet their needs. Within this personally designed plan, I discussed with them the long-term financial results of various employment scenarios. Their new plan provided a written financial road map which brought peace of mind in the midst of uncertainty.

~ Advisor Travel Tip: ~

Life can bring sudden changes with little warning. Having a tailored, written financial plan allows you to take a fresh look at where you are today, where you want to go, and how to get there.

Joyce, 70
Overwhelmed with Settling Her Husband's Estate

Joyce, a tall, thin woman dressed exquisitely in a snappy lime green Ralph Lauren outfit, came to me as a referral after her husband passed away. Joyce explained, "My husband, Neil, handled the majority of the family finances, but now that he's passed on, it's up to me to do the right thing. Lately, I'm not so sure what the right thing is. It's all so overwhelming!"

As happens in so many families, Neil had assured his wife that things were "all set," and yet after his death there were so many decisions to be made regarding investments, insurance, taxes, cash flow, IRAs, and beneficiaries.

Joyce realized the family's financial affairs were now her responsibility and, quite simply, she was seeking professional advice, prudently realizing, as she put it, "two heads are better than one."

I'll not forget the first day Joyce walked into our office, struggling under the weight of a huge box of papers. She had so many questions. She often reminds me how she felt her burden was lifted, literally and figuratively, as soon as she handed everything over to me.

As with all of our clients, I listened intently while Joyce confided in me regarding her goals and concerns given her family's dynamics. Paperwork was filling Joyce's mailbox every day since her husband's death and she was flabbergasted at the amount of paperwork necessary to settle Neil's estate. Neil had several accounts with various firms and all required their own set of paperwork and a certified death certificate. The instructions for completing the necessary paperwork were simply (and understandably) not clear to Joyce. While Neil had clearly designated beneficiaries (no probate was needed) Joyce and I still spent countless hours gathering, completing, and organizing necessary paperwork in order to settle Neil's estate.

Joyce felt good about having her attorney and me work with her through this process. Over time, we coordinated and simplified her financial affairs. After several months of working together and discussing strategies for the future, Joyce and I met with her attorney to update her trust and other estate planning documents.

~ Advisor Travel Tip: ~

There is no need to feel overwhelmed by all the paperwork. Find someone to help you. I <u>still</u> get baffled by the ambiguous instructions I receive from the majority of financial firms. YIKES!! No wonder consumers are overwhelmed and unsure.

The value of hiring a professional to help her organize, review, and coordinate her financial affairs brought Joyce the advice and financial security she was seeking. Joyce shared, "I believe my husband would be proud of me."

Tom, 54, Karen, 52
Getting Serious About Planning the Future

Tom, a stocky guy with handsome dark eyes and an orthodontist's dream of a perfect smile, came to our office with his sparkly eyed wife Karen looking for advice.

"We've both climbed the corporate ladder and between us have accumulated relatively significant wealth," Tom said. His tone of voice told me he wasn't bragging, just stating a fact.

What was the problem then, I wondered.

Karen broke in. "The truth is, now that we're in our fifties we've come to an interesting crossroads. We're in our third showcase home, complete with lots of bling-bling, and you'd think we'd be happy, but instead we both feel like something is missing. The corporate life just isn't what either of us dreamed it would be," she said.

The sparkle I saw in Karen's eyes minutes before turned flat as she looked from her husband to me with a shrug of her shoulders.

During our meeting, I learned that this attractive couple, who had everything material, wanted our help to make sure their finances wouldn't be impacted too severely if they decided to scale back on their hectic work-centered lifestyle.

Throughout the planning process that followed, Tom and Karen confirmed that the trappings of success weren't worth the trade-off in terms of the loss of freedom to enjoy other interests including the great outdoors, meaningful relationships, and the things they had accumulated. They realized their need for instant gratification and "keepin' up with the Joneses" was taking a toll on their personal lives.

As we focused on their dreams and began designing a customized financial plan, both Tom and Karen began to see the long-term benefits of making values-based financial and life decisions. The written financial planning process helped Tom and Karen chart a different, more rewarding, purposeful course – something they desperately desired for their future.

~ Advisor Travel Tip: ~

An experienced advisor can help you evaluate what is truly important to you, ensuring you are focusing your financial plans on <u>values-based</u> goals and dreams.

Bob, 57, Connie, 56
Loving Husband Plans Ahead

One morning I got a phone call from Bob, a hard-working man employed for more than 30 years at a local corporation. He told me his co-worker and dear friend Joe had passed away suddenly after being diagnosed with cancer.

"Quite frankly, I'm tired of working, the clock is ticking and life is uncertain," Bob said. "What happened to Joe made me realize I've worked too hard to not be able to enjoy my retirement years. People give a company the best, healthiest years of their lives... for what?... And then they die."

Determined to change the direction of his life, Bob interviewed several financial advisors, seeking to hire the "right" person for the job. The final decision hinged on finding someone with whom his wife, Connie, could relate. Throughout their long marriage she'd never felt comfortable discussing their financial affairs. Therefore, it was of utmost importance to Bob to find a professional with whom Connie would feel comfortable, especially since, according to statistics, she would likely outlive him. If that happened, he didn't want her to be left without support to handle the family's financial matters.

Bob and I agreed it was important for Connie to meet with me even though she seemed disinterested and willing to abdicate all financial decisions to Bob. It was a loving gesture on Bob's part to take the time to find an advisor with whom his wife would feel comfortable. Conversely, it was a loving gesture on Connie's part to trust her husband so explicitly.

Sadly, three years later, Bob suddenly passed away. Though heartbroken, Connie appreciated and found comfort in the loving legacy her husband left, demonstrated by the care he took to involve her in organizing and coordinating their financial affairs. The transition to "being in charge" of the family's financial matters was manageable because

Connie had peace of mind knowing I would continue to serve her financial needs with respect and integrity.

If you are married, what would you do if your spouse became incapacitated or died tomorrow? Would you be in a position to suddenly "take charge" and make decisions, or does the thought concern you?

If you are single, who would take over and prudently manage your financial affairs if you were incapacitated or if you passed away? Would the person you chose be equipped for the role you are asking them to fill? Do they have the training and time it takes to engage in such an important role?

Because I have witnessed so many families dealing with sudden death or incapacitation, I am resolute in believing that a written financial plan, worked out ahead of time with a knowledgeable professional, is paramount to heading off hasty, and sometimes just plain wrong, decisions.

~ Advisor Travel Tip: ~

I have great respect and admiration for husbands and wives who take the time to find just the right financial professional to meet their family's needs. Of special importance to Bob was finding a professional his spouse felt comfortable with. Both partners had greater peace of mind knowing that if anything happened to one or the other, the surviving spouse would be provided for.

Help Wanted: Hiring a Professional Planner

"It costs money to live. I cannot simply dream a big dream, I need to plan financially to achieve what is important to me."

– Alice, 61

"Worrying about your financial affairs is like living life with your brakes on. You are constantly worried and unsure."

– Dorothy, 60

At this point you may be wondering what makes me qualified to advise you on how to hire the best financial help.

Over the years, I have advised hundreds of women in various circumstances – single women, widows, women who came in with their husbands or adult children, and women referred by their accountant or attorney.

One of the many reasons I felt passionate about writing this book was that I wanted to help women who were tired of running from one professional to another. Trying to find the best fit, many of these women were left on hold, figuratively and literally, waiting for someone, anyone, to give them straight answers.

Simply put, women appreciate working with someone with whom they can make a real heartfelt connection. They want an expert who, besides being straightforward and reliable, will talk with them face-to-face to help them put together all the unique pieces of their financial puzzle.

"In Malaysia, to call yourself a financial planner, you must be qualified, such as earning the local equivalent of the CFP® or the chartered financial consultant designation. But in the U.S, to hang out a shingle as a financial advisor, all you need is a shingle and a place to hang it."

– Wall Street Journal, May 31, 2006

Especially since the emergence of the Internet, there's plenty of free advice floating around, as well as many so-called "experts" willing to share their advice for a low, low price or even free!! But at what ultimate cost?

Bankers, brokers, insurance agents, financial advisors, investment advisors, and financial planners – they all may have sound advice, but if you don't select the *right* person who understands your unique journey, the process of designing a financial plan that meets your needs can leave you more confused, disheartened, and jaded then ever.

"I thought all a financial advisor would do is listen to my goals and then buy investments for me for a commission."

– Gloria, 47

I recommend you stay away from the "expert" who provides only isolated services, and look instead for a professional who advocates comprehensive financial and investment planning.

Chosen wisely, the *most highly qualified* financial professionals will first and foremost seek to build a **relationship** with you based on **mutual respect** and understanding. Working as a consultant, your advisor should take the time to **listen carefully** to your concerns in order to **design a unique written financial plan** that takes into consideration your values, emotional needs, dreams, and end-of-life wishes.

Besides building a strong rapport with you, your financial professional should provide *objective* advice and keep you abreast of current market conditions, interest rates, tax laws, and estate laws. It's his or her responsibility to explain in clear terms how each of these areas will impact your finances and how you can benefit from current trends.

If chosen wisely, your advisor should meet or exceed your expectations with unsurpassed quality guidance and service. Simply stated, they will put all the pieces of your financial puzzle together into one comprehensive, values-based plan for the future.

You may think of your financial professional as a travel guide who will point out areas of interest along the way as well as help you avoid pitfalls. It's your advisor's job to:

~ Provide you with a hassle free, enjoyable experience
~ Develop a "travel itinerary" that will enable you to accomplish your goals
~ Help you "weather" possible travel plan interruptions
~ Coordinate your itinerary with other service providers (accountants, attorneys, and other professionals)

I strongly believe you should look for a professional who will provide you with a written *road map* directing you toward your goals, a place where you'll devote time to what matters most to you, and spend the rest of your life fine-tuning the legacy you wish to develop and leave for others on your *50&Forward* journey.

If hiring a financial professional still seems overwhelming, remember I'm taking this journey with you and I'm determined to be a good traveling companion. Hopefully, having a consultative financial advisor by your side will bring you satisfaction, so you'll feel confident to sit back and enjoy the journey with your speed limit set comfortably at *50&Forward* speed.

Imagine finding a financial professional who understands your unique situation and is mindful of what's most important to you. Now imagine this advisor prudently orchestrating a written financial plan designed just for you – carefully integrating your goals and dreams into your financial plan. Would this type of relationship help you feel more assured and confident? Would you feel a sense of control and peace of mind regarding your financial future?

Many women who realize the benefits of hiring a financial professional still feel ill-equipped, maybe even intimidated, by the notion of interviewing and questioning potential financial advisors.

Perhaps you can relate to the women I've profiled and realize the value in hiring a professional financial advisor for your *50&Forward* journey. Whether you are a novice or a financially savvy woman, you'll find that an experienced and well-qualified professional can be of tremendous value in managing your financial affairs.

As I have said, finding the right "fit" and having a quality relationship are of utmost importance to women. Since there is no such thing as "one size fits all" when it comes to finding the professional that's right for you, I recommend you engage in a bit of legwork before making your choice. Allow me to explain…

Five Powerful P's in a Pod...

1. Professionalism
2. Philosophy
3. Price
4. Product
5. Personal Style

Another one of my reasons for writing this book is to simplify the process of finding and working with a financial professional. I don't want you to feel intimidated. On the contrary, I want you to feel empowered! Keep in mind that most financial advisors will take the time to offer a free no-obligation consultation. Toward that purpose, I will provide you with some simple questions to ask prospective candidates, keeping in mind that the financial professional you choose should be one who gives you straightforward, easy-to-understand answers.

If you were traveling by car, you might turn to AAA for a road map and itinerary. However, on this trip I want you to consider the "Five Powerful Ps in a Pod," the five "must haves" I believe every professional financial advisor should provide and offer: Professionalism, Philosophy, Price, Product, Personal Style.

Feel free to take this book with you as a guide. It will come in handy as you interview prospective financial professionals. I have provided room at the end of this chapter for you to take notes to review later. Beware of making quick decisions. Remember, even the most wonderful and relaxing adventures take careful planning.

1. Professionalism

"The Certified Financial Planner™ or CFP® designation is considered the gold standard in this crowd. CFPs are required to be knowledgeable about financial planning topics including insurance, employee benefits, investments, taxes, and retirement and estate planning."
– Wall Street Journal, January 29, 2006

For starters, you may want to consider a financial professional with a CFP® certification. In many instances brokers, bankers, insurance agents, financial professionals, financial planners or even financial advisors don't have the knowledge and proficiency of a CERTIFIED FINANCIAL PLANNER™ practitioner. Many of them are simply product salespeople and offer isolated services.

A CERTIFIED FINANCIAL PLANNER™ practitioner is someone who will help you organize and coordinate all of your financial affairs and work very closely with the other professionals who represent you, including your attorney, accountant, CPA, insurance agent, and banker. They have extensive training in all six areas of comprehensive planning, including financial position, investment planning, insurance planning, retirement planning, tax planning, and estate planning.

"To ensure your advisor is knowledgeable, stick with CFPs or, alternatively, folks who have qualified to be chartered financial consultants, chartered financial analysts or certified public accountants – personal financial specialists."
– Wall Street Journal, May 31, 2006

Be sure to ask the financial professionals you interview:

~ If they are CFP® practitioners
~ What other credentials they have and what steps were required to earn those credentials
~ Their potential conflicts of interest
~ Areas of specialization (i.e., college planning, retirement planning, etc.)
~ How long they have been practicing

Be aware of "financial professionals" who have special titles attached to their names. Some companies award fancy sounding titles based on sales, production and/or company-sponsored short courses. For example, titles like "Vice President," "Investment Professional," and "Chartered Wealth Advisor" all sound good but what do these titles really mean and how are they earned?

If the person you are considering hiring has a designation or certification, be sure to ask about the basis or criteria for earning that recognition. For instance, was it awarded based on sales and production levels or completion of a simple company-sponsored class? Or was it earned through the advisor's demonstration of knowledge and skill?

Remember, the goal is to find someone who offers customized financial planning not isolated services. The areas covered typically include evaluating your current financial position, insurance and risk management, investment planning, tax planning, retirement planning, and estate planning. Many CFP® professionals are also highly specialized in specific areas and may be willing to work with you on a particular issue on a case by case basis.

Either way, it makes sense that their training, background, and continuing education be in comprehensive planning. The CFP® certification is a mark of assurance that the person you are interviewing is trained in comprehensive financial planning. A CFP® certificant is also required to complete bi-annual continuing education to keep his or her certification.

That being said, I am aware of a few people in the financial business who deliver outstanding advice and ongoing service without having the CFP® certification. However, the work of a financial professional practicing without a credible professional mark can be highly inconsistent. The benchmark of well-qualified financial advisors is the CFP® certification.

In addition, it also helps to have a well-tenured expert with several years of experience working with you.

~ Advisor Travel Tips: ~

~ If you desire to know more about a professional certification or want to understand what a certain mark means, go to the FINRA (Financial Industry Regulatory Authority) investor website at www.finra.org. Select "investor information". Then select "professional designations".

~ To ensure you are hiring someone knowledgeable, search for a CERTIFIED FINANCIAL PLANNER™ practitioner at www.CFP.net.

~ To check disciplinary action or to confirm your CFP® is in "good standing," contact the CERTIFIED FINANCIAL PLANNER™ Board of Standards at 1-888-237-6275 or www.CFP.net. This group establishes, monitors, and enforces the standards CFPs must meet in order to call themselves CFP® practitioners.

~ For a list of CERTIFIED FINANCIAL PLANNER™ practitioners in your area contact the Financial Planning Association

National Planning support center at 1-800-647-6340 or www.FPANET.org then click "find a planner."

~ Consider looking into your financial professional's record before hiring him or her. A U4 is a record the FINRA keeps on every licensed financial professional in the country. Contact them at 1-800-289-9999 or log onto www.finra.com.

"I realize that a financial planner's background, expertise and services can vary greatly."

– Julie, 50

2. Philosophy

By asking the financial professionals you interview about their philosophy regarding financial advice and planning, you should get a feel for their level of commitment to clients and the financial planning process they follow.

Ask questions such as:

~ How frequently do you meet with your clients?
~ Is it **you** I'll be meeting with?
~ What is your investment philosophy?
~ What exactly do we talk about during review meetings?
~ What is delivered verbally and/or in writing?
~ Do you call me or do I have to call you regarding meetings and changes?
~ How do you keep track of clients, their investments, etc.?

"Only 59% of women met with or spoke over the phone with their financial advisor more than twice a year."
– Women's Institute on Aging

Because the financial planning process is ongoing and dynamic and the investment arena changes so quickly, most clients warrant a minimum of two scheduled, in-depth review meetings annually, ideally face to face, and at least one to three courtesy calls throughout the year. Depending on how well-trained the advisor's staff is, portions of your service may be delivered by qualified staff. Whatever your arrangement, it should be agreed upon in advance.

I'm often asked how a client knows when it's time to meet or make changes. Rest assured, proactive financial professionals consider it their job to contact you regarding appointments, portfolio changes, tax savings ideas, written financial planning updates, etc. It is not your job to contact them unless circumstances arise prompting additional questions or concerns. You should never have to wait and wonder. This is your journey and you deserve the best!

~ Advisor Travel Tip: ~

My philosophy includes educating clients to the extent they want to be educated. The reason is simple. I recognize that when I, as a consumer, receive advice or information from a doctor, dentist, contractor or other service provider, I tend to "zone out" if they deliver too much information, jargon or an abundance of detail. I go on overload! The same holds true with our clients. Feel free to ask as many questions as come to your mind. If there is a point you do not understand, ask your advisor to explain again using layman's terms.

3. Price

"The financial planning industry is like the secret underground. No one really knows how they make their money, but everyone knows they do."
— **Barb, 63**

Remember the story about the little red hen that found a few kernels of corn and wanted the other animals to help her make bread? None of them were interested in doing the work, but they all wanted a piece of the finished product when it came out of the oven.

Too often so-called "financial experts" are like the lazy animals in the children's story — they aren't particularly interested in rolling up their sleeves and doing the work, they just want to reap the rewards.

If you're like most women, you're probably wondering just exactly how financial professionals are paid and how much the products and services they offer will cost. Perhaps the bags you're packing for your **50&Forward** journey feel just a bit heavier as you contemplate the task of investigating a number of professionals before choosing the one you hope is right for you.

Research indicates most people are willing to pay a fair price for quality financial advice.** That being said, research also supports that consumers want complete and accurate disclosure concerning **how** their financial professional is compensated for their work.

Most clients are comfortable paying in one of three ways:

**The Oechsli Institute

1. Paying a fee for written comprehensive financial planning and advice.
2. Paying a percentage – often based on assets invested.
3. A combination of 1 and 2.

So...why would you pay a fee for written comprehensive financial planning? Perhaps this analogy will help:

The financial planning process is actually quite similar to the experience I had in my desire to schedule an appointment for myself with a physician who had been referred to me. Understandably, the administrative assistant informed me I would need to schedule a complete physical with the doctor before he would take me as a new patient. Personally, I appreciated his desire to get the comprehensive picture of my medical history and current health. I eagerly scheduled an appointment for the physical. Before undergoing my physical, the doctor took the time to help me understand his new patient policy. This reassured me that he had my best interest in mind and would provide quality health care to meet my needs.

Similar to the doctor's new patient policy, the financial planning process also includes a "complete financial physical." Typically when a client meets with a CFP® practitioner, a series of meetings are scheduled in an effort to get a comprehensive picture of the clients' financial health including the facts surrounding their current financial situation, cash flow, net worth, insurance coverage, risk exposures, estate plans, retirement plans, and income taxes.

It's also important for the financial professional to understand their clients' goals, dreams, and thoughts regarding life, family, charity, health, etc. The financial professional you hire cannot perform his or her best for you unless you are completely open and honest. By fully understanding the dynamics of your situation, they are better equipped to put all the puzzle pieces together into a quality comprehensive plan that's right for you.

Typically, the investment a client makes to go through the comprehensive written financial planning process with our practice ranges from $800 – $2,500. Based on feedback from clients through the years, this fee was a small investment compared to the benefits provided.

After a new client completes the initial comprehensive financial planning process, if suitable and appropriate, we discuss options regarding how we are paid for our <u>ongoing</u> advice and service.

Many clients choose to pay a set fee based on assets invested. In the industry, this type of an arrangement is generally referred to as a "wrap" account. The fee is negotiable and may vary based on the dollar amount of assets held in the account, the activity level within the account, the complexity of the investment strategy, and the frequency of meetings and additional contacts. This fee averages between 0.5% and 2.5% annually. When you are working with an advisor and choose this route, you will also want to discuss any **internal hidden** costs within each investment held inside the wrap account. In our practice, we help clients understand how the wrap account works. We also explain that our goal is to keep the *overall* cost to the client low by selecting cost effective investments within the wrap account.

Under the wrap account structure, financial professionals typically do not receive commission for buying and selling investments. Rather, they have an incentive to drive up the value of your portfolio or, in a down market, reduce losses. Another benefit to the client is that the fee you are paying is transparent – it is not hidden.

I prefer this method (when appropriate for the client) as do our clients. Having a clear understanding of how the advisor is compensated, and at what percent, allows clients to see what value they are receiving now, and on an ongoing basis, for the fee they are paying.

"How can you have peace of mind when you know your relationship is driven by commission?"

– Jan, 63

Shirley, 60, Bill, 58
Finding the Right Fit

Shirley and Bill, small business owners, hired our practice to manage half of their sizeable investment portfolio. The other half was being managed by a broker whose quality of customer service was diminishing. Being loyal clients, Shirley and Bill found it difficult to sever the ties with their broker and I respected their viewpoint.

During our scheduled review meeting, I recommended Shirley and Bill make a few changes to rebalance their portfolio based on our established Investment Policy Statement (IPS), Asset Allocation modeling, current market conditions, and their goals. Shirley and Bill were pleased with our service and felt we addressed their specific needs and goals during our review. They also felt comfortable because they understood how we were compensated for the services provided to them. They understood they were paying a percentage (based on invested assets) for the advice and services we delivered. Because they knew we did not work on commission, they weren't left to question our motives for recommending certain changes.

A few weeks after our meeting with Shirley and Bill, their broker called to recommend several changes. This was the first phone call to them in over a year and a half. During their meeting, the broker recommended Bill and Shirley sell four stocks, four stock funds, and two bond funds and buy six other new investments.

Bill and Shirley explained to their broker that they would need to go home and think about his recommendations. They then contacted me that same day to inform me of their uncomfortable feeling.

Shirley explained, "We had not heard from or seen this guy in over a year and a half and suddenly he had all of these recommendations. How could we know for sure that he was representing our best interests, not his?"

While I don't believe it is "wrong" for a client-focused professional to work on commission, assuming suitable and appropriate investment recommendations are made, I believe that in today's investment world, consumers view fee-based planning as an increasingly comfortable option. In my viewpoint, working on commission is simply a bit antiquated.

~ Advisor Travel Tips: ~

~ The method of payment for services rendered should be made clear up front and not left to question. You should not be left wondering how your hired professional is paid for his or her services.

~ As the old saying goes, "don't be penny wise and pound foolish." You'll receive tremendous value for the fees you pay to a reputable and qualified financial professional, provided you ask good questions like the ones I suggested earlier in this chapter. Keep in mind that the best, most reputable financial professionals are not likely to be the cheapest, nor are they likely to be available for an initial meeting the week you call.

~ A reputable, well-qualified financial professional with a high level of experience will naturally attract favorable attention in your area. Ask a respected attorney, accountant, family member or friend for a recommendation and make sure the advisor specializes in *comprehensive* financial planning. And again, consider hiring a CFP® practitioner – your best bet when it comes to choosing a financial professional you'll be happy with for life.

4. Product

It's important to ask the prospective financial professionals you are interviewing if they offer the most up-to-date financial investment products available in the market today. Because investments are the building blocks for designing your portfolio, I recommend choosing an objective professional who offers all types of investments. Additionally, the financial professional you decide to work with should not be limited to offering only proprietary products (products produced and sold exclusively by his or her firm).

To best meet your unique and individual needs, your financial professional should offer nearly all types of stocks, bonds, mutual funds, index funds, ETFs, certificates of deposit, annuities, REITS, and more. These product offerings should be extensive, enabling him or her to objectively offer and recommend the investments and programs most appropriate for you.

There have been brokerage firms and financial institutions known to recommend, and even push, a particular stock or other investment because their brokers and representatives were offered bonuses or incentives for selling them. I'm sure you'll agree this hardly seems ethical. How can a professional act in your best interest given this structure? Be sure you understand how your advisor makes investment selections and where the research comes from.

Forrest, 71, Louise, 69
Looking for Options to Meet Our Needs

Forrest, standing a tall six-foot-two, and Louise, a petite five-foot-four with heels, were referred to us by a long-time client. Over the phone, Louise explained that they wanted a second opinion regarding some mutual funds they had invested in. The funds just didn't seem to be performing as well as they should be.

We scheduled a meeting, and after reviewing their statements and doing a bit of research, I discovered Forrest and Louise had nearly all their retirement dollars invested in three different annuity products offered by one life insurance company.

It became apparent after talking with them that their current "financial advisor," an insurance representative working on commission, had placed Forrest and Louise in one of the limited insurance products offered by his firm.

Furthermore, Louise and Forrest had no idea how they paid for the advice, if the "advisor" was paid, and if they were paying any internal fees. The answers were "yes" the advisor received high commissions up front and "yes" the internal hidden fees were comparatively high.

During my tenure as a CFP® certificant, I have met and worked with many people like Forrest and Louise with similar concerns. Unfortunately, their situation isn't uncommon. Implementing simple steps and completing some legwork, along with asking good questions, will help to avoid a compromising situation.

~ Advisor Travel Tip: ~

I recommend finding a financial professional who objectively offers a wide variety of investments and options to meet your unique needs.

5. Personal Style

Chemistry is critical. First impressions are typically accurate. Many women have shared with me that they could tell fairly quickly if the connection with a prospective advisor was "right" or "wrong." I encourage you to let your "woman's intuition" guide you, keeping in mind that, if chosen wisely, your financial professional will most likely be your ally for life.

As soon as possible after meeting with a prospective financial professional, find a comfortable spot, maybe a coffee house or favorite restaurant, and jot down your impressions regarding what was said and how the person made you feel. It's important to do this as soon as is practical since much of your recall will be lost if you wait too long. Think back over your conversation and ask yourself:

~ Was the setting comfortable and inviting?
~ Did I feel at ease?
~ Did the person seem sincerely interested in what I was sharing?
~ Is he or she someone I could be open and honest with?
~ Would my children like this person?
~ Was he or she an active listener?
~ Did this person exude confidence in his or her work?
~ Did he or she project a friendly nature?
~ Did it seem this person was passionate and committed to his or her work?
~ Was this person enthusiastic?
~ Would my family be comfortable dealing with this person now and in the future?
~ Did it feel like I was being "sold"?
~ Did this person speak to me on my level?
~ Did he or she intimidate me with financial jargon?

~ Did he or she treat staff and co-workers with respect and dignity?

Well, ladies, I trust the "5 Powerful Ps in a Pod" will help you find your way along the *50&Forward* highway. In summation, after you've completed your legwork, asked the right questions, and you're satisfied with a prospective financial professional's **professionalism**, **philosophy**, range of **products**, **price**, and **personal style**, you will have arrived at the threshold of a very valuable relationship.

Remember, your comfort level should grow along with the relationship you build with your financial professional. Who you choose is strictly up to you and you have every right to terminate your relationship with your advisor if you're not satisfied, better yet delighted, with his or her advice and service.

I hope I've helped you understand how valuable a CERTIFIED FINANCIAL PLANNER™ practitioner or other financial professional can be during your *50&Forward* journey. I also hope these insights will help you feel more comfortable, confident, and better equipped to interview and hire the best person to accompany you on this exciting adventure.

Financial Freedom: Driving the 50&Forward Highway

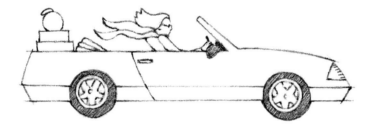

"A successful financial planning relationship has everything to do with your relationship. You must feel confident and comfortable with your hired professional."

– Jenna Everett, CFP®

Think of your financial professional as your well-equipped tour guide and traveling companion – someone who is there for you as you journey forward. Like myself, most advisors derive great joy and satisfaction in observing their clients plan for their dreams, pursue their lives with passion and purpose, and develop a living, loving legacy for the people they hold dear.

At this juncture, you should feel comfortable enough to continue sharing what a favorite attorney of mine calls "the good, the bad, and the ugly." I like that! Just as a doctor won't be able to look after you if you don't tell him or her everything, neither will the financial professional you've hired be able to help you make plans for the future if he or she doesn't understand you completely.

Be prepared upon meeting with your new financial professional to present:

~ Financial statements
~ Cash flow statements, if available
~ Tax returns
~ A list of assets and liabilities
~ Retirement planning information
~ Estate planning documents
~ Goal clarification
~ Thoughts regarding your dreams and passions
~ Family and/or charitable desires
~ Information regarding your family dynamics

Your financial professional will then be able to develop a customized financial plan designed just for you. Think of it as a road map based on the facts surrounding your situation combined with careful attention to your goals, dreams, and lifestyle desires. That's why it's so critical to work with an advisor who is an active, attentive listener!

One of the tools we provide for our clients is an organizational binder used to keep their financial information in one convenient location. We consider it our job to make sure the information in this binder is updated frequently. Many of our clients tell their families, "If anything happens, the black binder is in the file drawer. Just call the Everetts. They're familiar with all our financial stuff."

After careful analysis, your advisor will most likely arrange to meet with you several more times to discuss your financial and life plans. Discussions may include:

~ Refining your goals, based on your dreams and lifestyle choices
~ Analyzing your current financial situation
~ Prioritizing what you consider most important
~ Evaluating how well your current investments meet your goals, objectives, and income needs
~ Initiating an ongoing and dynamic step-by-step personalized plan
~ Analyzing how one decision impacts another
~ Analyzing cash flow projections
~ Creating an IPS (investment policy statement).
~ Customizing your investment strategies
~ Advice on specific investments
~ Monitoring of your investments
~ Coordinating with other professionals to help you benefit from changes in tax and estate laws
~ Devising a system to help you stay organized and coordinated
~ Developing a risk management plan that includes long-term care, disability, and life insurance
~ Continuous detailed, yet easy to understand, investment ideas
~ Rebalancing and optimizing your portfolio
~ Retirement planning, including projections and alternate scenarios
~ Estate planning tools and strategies to help you meet your legacy goals.

Like the ongoing financial planning process, the relationship you have with your advisor should be ongoing as well. Let's face it; the only constant in life is change. As you've no doubt experienced many times, life is full of surprises. You can rest assured knowing your financial professional is right there with you to help each step of the way.

As you can see, this process is driven by a variety of ideas and considerations. Once your customized, values-based plan is implemented, it's a process that will continue year after year. It's my hope that as you find peace of mind working with your chosen financial professional, the relationship you have with him or her will grow into a sincere friendship.

This is about your quality of life and choosing not to leave your future happiness and sense of fulfillment purely to chance. Lack of planning is what keeps many people "stuck" with financial burdens and constant worry about the future. I believe women who understand the importance of making good values-based financial choices are the champions of the *50&Forward* adventure and their legacy will be a positive, life-affirming example for future generations to follow.

Like staying at a quality resort or a five-star hotel, checking your heavy bags at the concierge's desk provides you with a sense of relief, freeing you to enjoy the trip. Working with the right financial professional on your *50&Forward* journey can provide you with the same sense of relief. With a renewed "can do" outlook, a sense of empowerment, and peace of mind, you'll be equipped and ready for your exciting future.

My Money...

Points to Ponder...

My Money...

Points to Ponder...

_____

_____

_____

_____

_____

_____

_____

_____

_____

_____

_____

_____

_____

_____

_____

_____

_____

_____

_____

_____

_____

_____

_____

My Life

Packing up the Past...

"One faces the future with one's past."
– Pearl S. Buck

Have you ever contemplated how the past has a way of revisiting the present – good or bad? Many times, it is unresolved issues that have the most negative impact on our lives. Sadly, many people never discover that their old learned ways of perceiving events and situations are being repeated with tragic results.

For nearly 20 years, I have been establishing relationships with women on the *50&Forward* journey. The conversations I have had, and the observations I have made over the years, have reinforced my belief that there is a strong emotional connection to money. In fact, often times before beginning the financial planning process with clients, it has been crucial for me to explore how their past experiences and perceptions continue to influence their day-to-day quality of life – and ultimately, how the past can impact the legacy they will leave for future generations.

My goal is to help you prepare for a fulfilling and rewarding adventure. So, as you join thousands of other women on your *50&Forward* journey, take a careful look at the items in your bags. I urge you to inventory what you have packed for your journey both consciously and unconsciously. I encourage you to pack lightly, realizing less is more. Simplicity is often the key to living intentionally and authentically.

You have spent 50 or more years of your life piecing together different experiences to arrive at this place in your life's journey. Whether good or bad, right or wrong, healthy or unhealthy, the items packed in your bags have influenced the choices you have made. If you are like most women, some of your decisions served you well and others are still holding you back, making it a struggle to move forward. Take a moment now to think back and revel in the many victories you've won and confront the losses you've overcome to grow stronger and wiser. It's time to celebrate your life!

Betty, 57
Creating a Balanced Lifestyle

Betty grew up on a rather large estate in an affluent neighborhood, not wanting for material things. Her well-to-do parents were often absent, working hard to lavish the family with expensive vacations, a showcase home, designer clothing, choice foods, her father's imported cigars, and other luxury items meant to provide happiness. This was the only lifestyle Betty knew.

As an adult, Betty found herself on the same fast track to success as her parents, both of whom had died relatively young from ill health, most likely stress-related, she now thinks.

As Betty and I began to talk, it became clear to her that the negative lifestyle choices her parents made had patterned the kind of life she herself was living. Nearing 40, she had begun to see in herself the same unhappy, negative, and unforgiving person that both her mother and father had become. Her family, the family who "had it all," really had nothing, Betty sadly realized. Thankfully, before she went on making the same mistakes, Betty decided to focus her energies on creating a more balanced lifestyle for herself and her family. She began making values-based decisions regarding her health, family, friends and finances.

Whatever experiences are included in your personal history, you have the opportunity to learn from your past. Taking an honest look at yourself and your past is crucial as you prepare for your journey ahead. Knowing yourself will equip you to pack with a plan and a purpose, allowing you to make good choices regarding the financial, physical, emotional, and spiritual items you will be including in your bags.

I personally invite you to acknowledge and own the wisdom you have gained as you examine your life's experiences and the decisions made, or not made, along the way. Ultimately, I believe this wisdom will allow you to live a more freeing and meaningful life and pass along valuable life lessons to those you love.

As the old song goes (and if you're over 50 you'll probably remember it) "You got to Ac-Cent-Tchu-Ate the positive, elim-inate the negative, latch on to the affirmative and don't mess with Mr. In-between."**

**Song: "Ac-Cent-Tchu-Ate the Positive" – Words by Johnny Mercer, Music by Harold Arlen

What Matters Most?

As you consider the next phase of your journey, consider taking a closer look at the lessons you've learned along the way.

Side Trip #3 Directions

1. For this exercise, find a comfortable place to work and pour yourself a cup of coffee or another beverage of your choosing.

2. I believe this exercise will provide you with the opportunity to acknowledge and explore who you are and what makes you the unique individual you are today. Don't worry if you don't have many memories in your mind or lessons for each of the four categories. I know this exercise may take some time and it should. This is your life...sometimes we don't know how that comfy red sweater or those "too snug" polka dot hot pants got into our suitcase.

3. To assist you in making this just a little easier, I have provided an example of a "Decades of Discovery" chart on pages 90-92. Please take a few minutes to review it.

DECADES OF DISCOVERY

VALUES

DECADE	Financial	Emotional	Physical	Spirituality
Early Years (birth-19)				
Age10 – Spending a special day with my grandpa, picking out my very first bike. I didn't sleep the night before. I was so excited. When we got to the Schwinn store, I had a tough choice to make between the green banana seat bike with one-speed, the fancy 3-speed sparkler and the basic – basket deluxe.	I chose the green banana seat, one-speed. I was just so excited!! Even though I could have had any bike I wanted, I chose to be careful of my grandfather's money. I chose the basic one – speed bike because I thought it was probably the best deal.	I learned how significant and meaningful it is when someone gives of his or her time to make you feel special.	Because I took such pride in my special bike, I took very good care of it and I rode it a lot. It made me feel good.	Looking back, I realize I was learning a valuable life lesson. It is truly better to give than to receive.
	LESSON: I learned it's not about the biggest and the best.	**LESSON:** It is important to make time for others.	**LESSON:** Being active and doing things I like makes me feel good.	**LESSON:** Giving makes life worth living.

DECADE	VALUES			
	Financial	Emotional	Physical	Spirituality
20's Age 27 – Recently separated and financially strapped, I decided to take on a part-time summer teaching position to make ends meet. I was both emotionally and physically exhausted. Realizing I was unable to give my students my all, I resigned at the end of the first week. When I informed my supervisor of my decision he expressed his approval by telling me he was proud of me for making a good decision to take care of myself.	Making good choices about where to spend my money and energy allowed me to regain my health and perspective. Less than a month later I applied for a position that allowed me to pursue a new career in program development while also increasing my income. **LESSON:** Money is a means to an end.	My emotional health was more important than a job. **LESSON:** My career is not my whole identity. It is only one part of who I am.	My physical health was more important than a job. **LESSON:** It is OK to quit when my health is compromised.	I knew I needed to step out in blind faith and trust that God would provide for my needs. Just as God instructed Abraham to go blindly in faith, I too, had the privilege of letting go of my circumstances, trusting God would make a way. **LESSON:** Let go and let God.

DECADE		VALUES		
	Financial	Emotional	Physical	Spirituality
30's Age 32 – In the 1970s on the street where we lived, it was common to socialize with the neighbors. Because it was convenient, I began to have more parties and drank more. I remember one night I had intentions of having one drink; instead, I drank the whole bottle and blacked out. I realized I was out of control and couldn't stop at just one drink. My family admitted me to rehab and it was there I learned I had crossed the line from "social drinking" to alcoholism. As a result, I chose to attend Alcoholics Anonymous (AA)	I was a mother of four, on a limited budget, yet the first things in my grocery cart were whiskey, vodka, gin, and Newports. **LESSON:** It costs money to support bad habits. **LESSON:** "If you are going to dance, you have to pay the fiddler." My father was right.	As I faced my divorce I became distraught thinking about raising four children on my own. I began to doubt myself and my abilities. I thought my family would be better off without me. **LESSON:** I realized I was at the height of self centeredness. **LESSON:** Compromising my values is not worth the expense.	While in rehab I examined my life more closely and came to the realization that alcoholic tendencies were evident in my family history. **LESSON:** It is important to know your family medical history and pass it along to your loved ones.	Turning to crutches and vices is not a solution. They cannot bring lasting peace of mind. They merely numb the pain temporarily. **LESSON:** Putting God first in all things brings lasting peace and fulfillment.

4. Now it's your turn. It's time to look back on the different decades in your life, including:

~ early years (1 – 19)
~ 20s
~ 30s
~ 40s
~ 50s
~ 60+

For each decade, think about a particularly poignant experience. Can't remember anything significant? I suggest digging out the ole photo albums, calling a friend or family member or playing some oldies as you begin reminiscing.

I encourage you to take your time, look at your life, and celebrate all you've become.

To get you started I have provided blank charts on the following pages for you to begin recording your own "Decades of Discovery."

Take your time. You owe it to yourself. We will be referring back to this later.

DECADES OF DISCOVERY

DECADE	VALUES			
	Financial	Emotional	Physical	Spirituality
Early Years (birth-19)				
	LESSON:	LESSON:	LESSON:	LESSON:

DECADE	VALUES			
20s	Financial	Emotional	Physical	Spirituality
	LESSON:	LESSON:	LESSON:	LESSON:

DECADE	VALUES			
30s	Financial	Emotional	Physical	Spirituality
	LESSON:	LESSON:	LESSON:	LESSON:

DECADE	VALUES			
40s	Financial	Emotional	Physical	Spirituality
	LESSON:	LESSON:	LESSON:	LESSON:

VALUES				DECADE
Spirituality	Physical	Emotional	Financial	50s
LESSON:	LESSON:	LESSON:	LESSON:	

DECADE	VALUES			
	Financial	Emotional	Physical	Spirituality
60 +				
	LESSON:	LESSON:	LESSON:	LESSON:

Living with Forgiving

"To forgive is to set a prisoner free and discover the prisoner was you."

– Unknown

Tragically, over the years I've known clients and many other women and men who have chosen to carry the weight of anger and hurt into what should be the most fulfilling time of their lives. I've witnessed the horrible consequences of letting resentment form the basis of financial decisions and life choices.

I believe living without forgiving is not really living at all. It's not only liberating to forgive, it's healthy. As your tour guide, I feel so passionately about the importance and power of forgiveness that I've devoted several pages to it.

Frequent flyers know the journey is a lot easier, and less expensive, without excess baggage. I've had the privilege of working with, and knowing, people who intentionally chose the path of forgiveness and restoration. Many of them experienced for the first time the freedom that comes with forgiving, and as a result, experienced some of the most eye-opening, spiritually awakening scenery along life's journey.

In the last exercise, "Decades of Discovery," you looked at significant experiences that impacted your life and taught you valuable financial, emotional, physical, and spiritual lessons. While completing this exercise you may also have identified relationships where forgiveness needs to take place. Perhaps you need to forgive someone or you need to ask someone to forgive you. Maybe the person who most needs forgiveness from you is you!

Let's face it, we have all said or done things, intentionally or unintentionally, that have hurt others. During stressful situations in our lives, emotions run particularly high. These times might include dynamics around death and funerals, marriage, divorce, financial hardship, job loss, and other family dynamics and family situations.

> *"You gain strength, courage, and confidence by every experience in which you really stop to look fear in the face. You must do the thing which you think you cannot do."*
> **– Eleanor Roosevelt**

Forgiveness is letting go, sometimes without necessarily knowing why someone wronged you. Forgiveness is also letting go of your own past regrets. It's about looking deep inside yourself and choosing to intentionally lighten your load so you have the energy and peace of mind to move forward.

We tend to think of forgiveness in terms of what it does for the other person as we free them from feelings of guilt or shame. Ironically, forgiveness is also about letting go of our own emotional baggage and focusing on our own journey. Without forgiveness the excess baggage can (and will!) be harmful to our health and well-being. Over the years, I have observed people who have lost the sparkle in their eyes and physically aged five – ten years in just a few short months due to the damaging effects of living without forgiving. I believe it is the spiritual equivalent of a climber with a 250-pound backpack attempting to experience the beautiful scenery of Mount Everest!

You cannot forgive others until you look inside yourself and unpack the toxic baggage you may have chosen to carry. Remember: true forgiveness starts by forgiving yourself and then reaching out to forgive others, whether or not they seek or deserve your forgiveness. Life is too short to live without forgiving.

*"Forgiveness is a funny thing.
It warms the heart and cools the sting."*

– William Arthur Ward

Forgiveness Forum

Side Trip #4 Directions

Try this exercise out loud. Pretend you're talking to a person, living or deceased, who hurt you; someone who in the past you've been unable or unwilling to forgive. (If it's yourself you need to forgive, it may help to sit in front of a mirror.)

Forgiving Someone Else:

When you _____ (name the action) it made me feel _____ because it said to me that you _____ _____ (fill in the motive you perceive the other person had).

Forgiving Myself:

When I _____ (name the action) it made me feel _____ because it said to me that I _____.

To get you started I have provided some examples on the following page:

Mary, age 45: Relationship with Critical Parent

When you <u>were critical of me</u>, you made me feel <u>like I could never measure up to your standards</u> because it said to me that <u>I was not lovable just for being me</u>.

Monica, age 60: Widowed with Unexpected Financial Hardship

When you <u>died suddenly and I discovered we were not financially "all set"</u> you made me feel <u>betrayed and unloved</u> because it said to me you <u>did not care enough about me to make sure I would be taken care of if you died</u>.

Joan, age 72: Mismanagement of Mother's Estate by Sibling

When you <u>spent mother's money for your own personal gain without consulting your siblings</u>, you made me feel <u>as if our mother's wishes weren't important and neither was our family</u>.

Judy, age 63: Forgiving <u>Herself</u> After Realizing She Mistreated Her Deceased Alcoholic Father

When I <u>treated my father like a nobody</u>, it made me <u>feel like I was a horrible person</u> because <u>I couldn't accept my dad for who he was</u>.

Now it's your turn: Create your own "forgiveness forum." Refer back to pages 104 & 105 if you need to.

Forgiving Someone Else:

When you _____

it made me feel _____ because it said to me

that you _____.

When you _____

it made me feel _____ because it said to me

that you _____.

When you _____

it made me feel _____ because it said to me

that you _____.

Forgiving Myself:

When I _____

it made me feel _____ because it said to me

that I _____.

When I _____

it made me feel _____ because it said to me

that I _____.

Now for the moment of truth...

Emotions can be very tricky, especially when you're confronted with a situation that's out of your control; for example, when you're under attack – verbally, emotionally or physically. The good news is, as any well-trained counselor would tell you, no one but you have control over your emotions and reactions. No one can <u>make</u> you feel anything without your consent. It is up to each of us to take responsibility for how we feel.

An emotional reacton or overreaction may sometimes be triggered by bad memories from some related, or maybe unresolved, incident in your past. How many of us have made "mountains out of molehills" and wondered why. Once you understand what is driving your feelings, you can make a choice to be intentional and deliberate about seeking forgiveness and letting go. The result will be emotional freedom and peace of mind.

Keeping in mind that no one can make you feel anything without your consent, let's revisit one of our examples and replace "you made me feel" with "I felt."

Mary, 45: Relationship with Critical Parent

When you <u>were critical of me</u> ~~you made me feel~~ <u>I felt afraid</u> because it said to me that <u>I was not lovable just for being me</u>.

Now it's your turn: When you are ready, revisit your statements on page 106 and replace "you made me feel" with "I felt." Using feeling words like angry, happy, scared, sad, etc. will allow you to embrace your true emotions and understand how to let go and forgive.

While discussing family dynamics with clients over the years, I realized many of them feel their situation is the "exception to the rule." Sometimes they go out of their way to convince me that the rift in their relationship(s) is the other person(s) fault. Or they'll insist that the wound the other person inflicted runs so deep, forgiveness is out of the question.

Or, if they acknowledge the fault was their own, they may believe they cannot be forgiven and, worse yet, they feel they can never forgive themselves.

Sometimes people pretend they have forgiven, but there's a catch: "I can forgive, but I cannot forget," they'll say. In other words, the relationship will not be restored – anger, stress, strain, tension, resentment and hurt remain. I ask you, then, did this person ever really forgive?

I know forgiving someone you feel has wronged you can be difficult, and forgiving yourself is perhaps even more challenging. But as your tour guide, I am not asking you to forget the lesson, but rather to let go of the resentment that has made its way into the baggage that is weighing you down. It is time to experience "living with forgiving!"

"It's a fact that it is much more comfortable to be in the position of the person who has been offended than to be the unfortunate cause of it."

– Barbara Walters

June, now 67
Forgiving with No Strings Attached

June, 50, and her brother Tom, 55, both felt wronged by the other. Tom, as executor of their mother's estate, said and did things that were very hurtful, unfair, and just plain wrong in June's eyes. Quite simply, June felt betrayed and taken advantage of. With her daughter's agreement, and after many tears were shed, June sent a letter to Tom explaining how she felt about him and his actions. Instead of seeking to understand June's feelings of anger and hurt, the letter made Tom furious.

The closeness they once shared as siblings continued to be compromised by this unresolved issue that came between them for eight long years. Though June attempted to seek restoration on a few occasions, Tom's choice, and his wife Ann's choice, was to continue packing their traveling bags with an excess of anger and resentment – and they demonstrated their desire to hang on tight.

At one point Tom, now age 61 with significant health issues, finally talked with June. June stated how sorry she was and Tom expressed his desire to forgive and restore their relationship. (June thought it nothing short of a miracle!) Tom even planned to meet June for breakfast the next day. The following morning Tom called June as planned but, for some reason, his position had changed and his desire to forgive was never demonstrated. He died a year later at the age of 62.

Unfortunately, at some point over the eight year rift, Tom told his family he did not want his sister June at his funeral. So, Tom and Ann's daughter delivered a message to June telling her that she was not welcome to attend her brother's funeral. Apparently Tom and/or Ann didn't think, or maybe even didn't care, about the legacy they were developing.

Ten more years have passed since Tom's death. Family continues to wonder what role Tom's wife Ann played, and still plays, in the decision not to forgive. Ann is building her own legacy of "living without forgiving."

The unresolved quarrel between June, Tom, and Ann is being passed down to future generations. Family members who remain have to deal with the choice to live (and die) without forgiving – a burden that will undoubtedly weigh heavily on their hearts for years to come. June's sister-in-law Ann continues to claim, "You (June and her children) are not my family." How sad! Hopefully, at some point, the choice will be made by the next generation to seek true heartfelt forgiveness and restoration.

June realizes she made a big mistake. She did not mean what she wrote out of hurt and anger. June also realizes she can't change the past. She remains hopeful for the future and has peace of mind knowing she has asked forgiveness and attempted to reconcile. I believe June is experiencing true freedom and is living victoriously!

While I realize there are always two, three or more sides to a story, the point of "travel logs" like June's is that, regardless of who is at fault and how strongly you feel about your position, forgiveness is always the best, healthiest choice.

Ladies, there is no faking heartfelt forgiveness. The truth is, lack of forgiveness takes its toll and causes us to live in bondage. It's a scriptural truth. You can fake it for a while on the outside but not on the inside. Living without forgiving makes the road longer, the hills higher, and the road map you leave behind harder to read. Why not make the journey for those you love a little easier, showing them the wise path you have traveled? I guarantee the scenery is breathtaking and the quality of life exhilarating. Today is the day to set yourself free!

I am no stranger to the struggles that come from living without forgiving. Choosing not to let go of my hurt created excess emotional baggage in my own life, and negative thoughts robbed me of the joy in daily living.

Faith and belief in the bible and what God's word teaches helped me let go of the baggage I was carrying around. Wherever you draw your inspiration and motivation, you will benefit by choosing to unburden your heart so you can truly be attentive to the joy-filled journey that lies before you. Seek to find the beauty in humankind, agree to disagree, and focus on the good in everyone.

"Forgiveness is letting go...no longer allowing negative thoughts and feelings to rent space in your head and your heart...no longer letting a grudge impact your financial and life decisions."

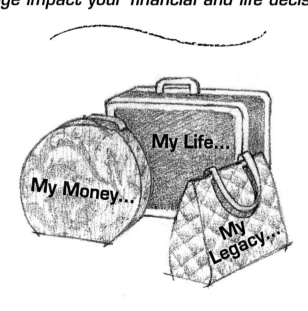

*"I know in my heart that man is good.
That what is right will always eventually
triumph. And there's purpose and
worth to each and every life."*

– Ronald Reagan

Living with Forgiving

Begin by being intentional and deliberate about your thoughts, words, and actions and their lasting impact on you and others. You may also want to consider what message an unforgiving life gives to the next generation. What will your legacy be?

Side Trip #5 Directions

1. Now it is your turn...Refer back to "Freely Forgiving" exercise on pages 103-107 and answer the following questions.

~ What relationship(s) needs mending?

~ What necessary meeting needs to take place before you journey forward?

~ What person do you need to talk with before your journey continues?

Now think of your legacy and the values you are leaving for others to discover – an easy-to-read road map with a clear route above the clouds where the sun is typically shining. The legacy of "living with forgiving" will continue for generations to come. What a gift to future generations as they follow in your footsteps and embark on their own unique journeys.

Ladies, today is the day to pursue "living with forgiving."

"To err is human; to forgive, divine."

– Alexander Pope

Dream

Daring to Dream: A Journey of Possibilities...

~ A possibility

~ A cherished desire

~ An aspiration

~ Something that fully satisfies a wish

~ A strongly desired goal

"Brilliant ideas may come to you while you're soaking in a hot bubble bath, but will you be one of the few who get out of the tub, dry off, and do something about their vision or idea?"

I believe God put a big dream in your heart. The good news is you already have the gifts and talents to pursue and accomplish your dream! For many of us, the pursuit of our dreams has yet to be fulfilled.

Working toward a dream can enrich your life and allow you to feel creative, connected, alive, free, young, fulfilled, and even daring! Without a dream, you may struggle to see potential in yourself because you don't look beyond your current situation or circumstances.

With a dream, you intentionally choose to see yourself in a new light, setting goals and desiring to do more...to be all you were created to be.

Do you have a dream tugging at your heartstrings? Are you one of the women who have come this far on the journey and realize you've put your dreams – both old and new – on hold? Today, it's your turn. As you begin your journey of possibilities, take this time to "be". Listen to your heart and in the quiet stillness you will find your innermost cherished desires and aspirations.

You may be thinking but...but...but...as the stack of life's demands pile up in your head. We aren't called the "sandwich generation" for nothing! Caring for those we love – the generations before us and the generations after us – can leave the *50&Forward* woman feeling overstretched and drained both physically and emotionally.

This is all the more reason for you to give priority to devoting time and attention to yourself and your dreams. As you ponder your dreams, remember that taking time to live your dreams will help you feel invigorated and better about yourself and your life. In fact, pursuing your dreams will quite possibly be a catalyst in helping you fulfill all of your life's roles with more energy and a healthier positive outlook.

What is your vision for the future? What have you always wanted to accomplish, but haven't? When you reflect upon your *50&Forward* journey, what will give you an **"I did it!"** sense of satisfaction? What are the possibilities? What steps do you need to take to make your dreams come true? What dreams need to be left behind? It's important to understand your dreams as your travel on your *50&Forward* journey.

A dream begins with an idea, a vision that grows out of a heartfelt desire and typically involves actions that are beyond our current experiences and comfort level. A dream can help us step outside of ourselves and honor parts of ourselves that we've let lie dormant or hidden over the years. Dreams allow us to reconnect with our deepest feelings and emotions.

While many people believe in the power of their dreams, there is a big difference between people who wish upon a star and people who choose to make their dreams come true. Brilliant ideas may come to you while you're soaking in a hot bubble bath, but will you be one of the few who get out of the tub, dry off, and do something about their vision or idea?

The forecast calls for sunny and 70 with no rain in sight. Ladies, it's a great day for a journey of possibilities! Let's grab a bite to eat at Erma's Diner and fill up at the Texaco before we head out. Rest assured – the benefits of this trip will be worth the price of a full tank of gas.

"Without leaps of imagination, or dreaming, we lose the excitement of possibilities. Dreaming, after all, is a form of planning."

– Gloria Steinem

"It is in hoping that we dream, in dreaming that we seek, in seeking that we find our life's desire."

– Unknown

Dream a Little Dream

I invite you to take your time in this section. If you have spent your life putting your dreams on hold, it may take some time for you to actually identify your dreams and understand why they're important to you. Your dreams deserve ample time for reflection. Take that time here.

Side Trip #6 Directions

1. Write down the dreams you currently have in your heart on page 125. To assist you I've included some examples below.
2. Why is pursuing this dream so meaningful to you?

Example:

Dream: To improve my health by losing weight and toning my body.

Why: I would feel a sense of satisfaction by attaining my health-related goal. I would also feel youthful, energized, and more self-confident.

Example:

Dream: To travel to England, Scotland, and Ireland.

Why: This trip would connect me to my family heritage. I would discover more about who I am. It would add excitement and possibilities to my life.

Example:

Dream: To own my own business.

Why: I would have the freedom to be my own boss, do meaningful work, and maintain a healthy balance between family and career.

"All our dreams can come true – if we have the courage to pursue them."

– Walt Disney

Dream:

Why:

Dream:

Why:

Dream:

Why:

Dream:

Why:

While advising clients during their **50&Forward** journey many shared their dreams, both fulfilled and unfulfilled, with me. Perhaps you will draw inspiration from their list of cherished desires and aspirations:

~ Spending time with grandchildren
~ Updating or remodeling a dream home
~ Growing a successful herb garden
~ Learning how to knit or crochet
~ Painting with watercolors
~ Taking a gourmet cooking class
~ Studying photography
~ Learning to play an instrument
~ Reading the classics
~ Learning a foreign language
~ Pursuing a college degree
~ Taking ballroom dancing
~ Learning yoga
~ Learning to race walk
~ Adventure cycling
~ Hiking and rock climbing
~ Sky diving
~ Running a marathon
~ Travel to exotic destinations
~ Joining the Peace Corps
~ Writing a screenplay
~ Writing a book

"The typical adventure traveler is not a 28-year-old male...it's a 47-your old female who wears a size 12 dress."

– Wall Street Journal, July 14, 2007

"I started organ lessons at the age of 50 after my first husband passed away. I have always regretted that I quit lessons after two years just because I got frustrated because I wasn't 'the best'...Oh how I wish I had not given up."

– Marilyn, 80

"So many times I began to pursue my dream, only to have 'life' get in the way. I look back now with regret that I did not seize the moment to follow my dreams."

– Mary, 73

Once you've identified your dream and the reason(s) *why* you want to pursue it, it's now time to set aside your fears, doubts, and feelings of inadequacy. Remember, there will always be someone who is better, faster or smarter than you. This is not about them – this is your dream. This is about following your heart and doing what's meaningful to you. Your dream can never be wrong, silly or inconsequential if it is truly authentic and heartfelt.

It's important to be deliberate about spending time with positive people who are living their dreams. Why not give those you trust and respect an opportunity to share your dream by painting a picture for them so they, too, can catch your vision? Their enthusiasm and encouragement will be a vehicle for helping you stay focused, accountable, and committed to living your dream. When you are willing to share your dream with others, the journey of possibilities becomes limitless.

As of the writing of this book, I have worked as a financial advisor for nearly 20 years. While I have felt blessed and honored to work with so many wonderful clients, I found myself searching for "something more." I was restless and knew there was more in God's plan for my life. Upon sharing my vision first with a colleague and then a client, each took the time to recommend powerful, life-altering books to me. These two books, *Half Time* by Bob Buford and *The Dream Giver* by Bruce Wilkinson drew me to contemplate my dream...my passion...and lead me to discover the path I was to take. My passion was ignited. The missing link was found! It became crystal clear that helping women live life intentionally and authentically, embracing their dreams and passions, and building a living, loving legacy was the avenue God had planned for me. My job was to step out in faith and do.

I called a dear and respected friend who I knew would help me pursue the dream before me – my journey of possibilities. Immediately, she validated my vision. In fact, she caught my excitement and vision. She encouraged me and expressed that "yes" dreams can, and do, come true. She and so many others propelled me toward my vision. The excitement and synergy was abundant. This is how *50&Forward* began, with women taking the time to listen, validate, and empower each other!

"Character cannot be developed in ease and quiet. Only through the experience of trial and suffering can the soul be strengthened, vision cleared, ambition inspired, and suggestion achieved."

– Helen Keller

In working toward my own dream, I confirmed my instinct...*meaningful* accomplishments take time and tenacity. I had been down this challenging "road to dreams" before, as a novice financial advisor at the age of 23. Yikes! One of the most powerful thoughts a dear woman from Texas shared with me at that time was, ***"There is nothing special about special people, it's what they do, not who they are."*** I took her comments to heart. I believed, and still believe, that if others can do it, I can do it! **I choose to believe in myself and the power of my dream.**

From the cathartic yet exhausting task of working toward my dream by authoring this book, I experienced my own ups and downs. Some of the feelings of fear and negative thoughts I had included: "Am I kidding myself, I'm not a writer! Who wants to read what I have to share?"

I was so excited and passionate one day and so ready to quit the next. The entire project seemed bigger than I had bargained for. The point is: dreams – meaningful, purposeful dreams – will not come easy. We must tenaciously keep our eyes on the goal and work toward it day by day, week by week, and month by month. **You** can do it! If anyone can, I know **you** can.

*"There is nothing special about special people,
it's what they do not who they are."*

*"Take chances, make mistakes. That's how you grow.
Pain nourishes your courage. You have to
fail in order to practice being brave."*

– Mary Tyler Moore

Living My Dreams

Through our experiences we find our dreams, dreams lead to possibilities, possibilities lead to passion, passion leads to purpose, purpose leads to fulfillment and fulfillment leads to meaning.

Side Trip #6 Directions

I invite you to experience the joy and personal satisfaction that comes from following your heart's desire. I believe pursuing your dreams will allow you to discover a part of yourself you've never known. Doing so will provide a more fulfilling journey. In addition, connecting with your innermost thoughts and desires will provide you with a canvas on which to design your living, loving legacy. Dreams may also serve as a catalyst for discovering your passion and purpose.

What have people told you you're good at?

What do you feel passionate about?

What small steps can you take today to begin reaching your dreams?

"The future belongs to those who believe in the beauty of their dreams."
— Eleanor Roosevelt

Passion:

~ Intense desire

~ Strong emotion

~ Boundless enthusiasm

Purpose:

~ What you are designed to do
(gifts and talents)

~ Guides your planned actions

~ Having meaning and significance

~ What something is used for,
function, role, intent

~ Justification of your existence

Finding Fulfillment: Living with Passion & Purpose

While gazing upon the horizon of your *50&Forward* years, trying to catch a glimpse of what your future might bring, have you ever felt like you were on board a cruise ship floating aimlessly without a charted course or an experienced captain at the helm?

Many women I've consulted with have expressed concerns about a lack of meaning and purpose which clouds their vision of the future. Whether they are talking about retirement planning or determining what to do with their time, too many of them are without a charted course.

> *"Some folks dream of the wonders they'll do, before their time on this planet is through...*
> *Some just don't have anything planned, they hide their hopes and their heads in the sand"**
> — **From the musical**
> **"Joseph and the Amazing Technicolor Dreamcoat"***

"Failing to plan is planning to fail."

— **Author unknown**

---

*Music by Andrew Lloyd Webber; Lyrics by Tim Rice

A cruise to nowhere may be an exciting and adventurous way to spend a few days, if that's truly your plan, but consider the women castaways of "Gilligan's Island," Ginger, Maryann, and Mrs. Howell, who couldn't wait to be rescued. Weekly episodes entertained us with ill-fated attempts to get off the island. A tropical paradise isn't much of a paradise if you feel as though you are "stuck" with no options. That's why it's so important to have a flexible plan that meets your needs and supports your goals for the future.

I find it interesting that the theme song for the show speaks of a "three-hour tour" aboard the "SS Minnow," yet Mrs. Howell, wife of millionaire Thurston Howell III, packed everything she thought she might "need." Obviously, she wanted to be prepared for any possible social opportunity that might present itself. You might remember Mr. Howell toting around her numerous bags packed with her expensive wardrobe, jewels, purses, make-up, and other accessories. While "Lovey" looked lovely in each episode, her wardrobe was of little benefit in helping her get off the island.

How can you live a meaningful life without engaging yourself in something meaningful? Check your bags. To make this voyage significant and satisfying, our itinerary calls for you to pack with a passion and a purpose.

Let's face it: if your life has become as predictable as sitcom reruns and you're looking for a little more passion and purpose, I invite you to book your cruise on the "SS *50&Forward*" cruise liner which offers several unique destinations. Together, we'll chart a course to your own personal paradise, wherever that may be. Your personal itinerary is guaranteed to include breathtaking scenery along the way. So, it is time to ask yourself...

What's My Passion? What's My Purpose?

Now, more than ever, women *50&Forward* are choosing to pack with passion and purpose. They seek to gain a greater understanding of who they are as they enter this new phase of their lives and discover what is meaningful to them. Women who find lasting purpose and fulfillment recognize the importance of being deliberate and intentional about the choices they make and how they spend their time. The choices they make will relate back to their passion and purpose and allow them to lighten their load by unpacking those extra outfits that won't be needed for the trip forward. Remember, ladies, as I mentioned before, there are very few role models – it's up to you to chart your own authentic course.

So, no more holding patterns! It's time to do and not just be! When you act with passion, you are more than a spectator hoping everything will turn out all right. Living with passion means assuming an active role in shaping and living the purpose of your life and not letting the winds of change simply blow you to and fro.

People who live their lives according to other people's expectations may never discover their true purpose for living. Others who know their purpose and don't act on it may wait too long to get started because they're waiting for inspiration, or permission, or an acorn to drop on their head. Who knows? But the time to get started is now. If not now, when?

Having difficulty identifying your passion? Turn back to pages 123 through 125 and revisit the exercise "Daring to Dream," pages 131 and 132 and revisit the exercise "Living My Dreams" and pages 93 - 99 to revisit the exercise "Decades of Discovery." Connecting the past with the present will get you started in the right direction and may even ignite your passion!

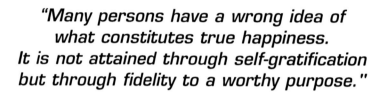

*"Many persons have a wrong idea of
what constitutes true happiness.
It is not attained through self-gratification
but through fidelity to a worthy purpose."*

– Helen Keller

Pat, 60
Overcame the Challenge of an Unhealthy Lifestyle and Inspired Others

The environment Pat grew up in was not conducive to good health by any means.

Her father was an alcoholic, her mother a chain smoker, and although there was always plenty to eat, the meals she and the rest of her family ate were consistently high in fat and calories. She jokes that when she was in college and missed her mom's cooking, all she had to do was head for the drive-through window at the closest hamburger joint.

Poor lifestyle choices took their toll on both her mother and father, who died at ages 60 and 59 respectively.

At age 40, Pat realized she was heading down the same slippery slope and taking her own family with her. It was at that point she made a commitment to implement important lifestyle changes, not only for her own sake, but for the sake of her children.

Nearly 20 years later, Pat is still intentional and deliberate about making healthy lifestyle choices. Her **passion** is an inspiration to many women desperately seeking to change their unhealthy lifestyles.In fact, her enthusiasm led to part-time employment where she continues to find purpose and fulfillment. Through pursuing her own passion by helping women work toward their lifestyle goals, Pat also helped these women discover their own unique passion and purpose. What a role model! What a legacy!

Pat shared, "It is a passion of mine to help others commit to healthy life choices."

Travel Log

Shirley, 68
Intense Desire to Give Back by Providing Grief Support

Shirley experienced tremendous grief over the loss of both of her parents to cancer. Throughout her time of hurting, she says what kept her going was the genuine kindness shown to her by caring people who would not let her grieve alone.

Their loving support meant so much to Shirley that she decided to give back to other families experiencing the same devastating grief and suffering that comes from losing a loved one to cancer. Because of her **intense desire** to give back, Shirley began volunteering with her local hospice organization and eventually went through training to become a grief counselor.

Shirley's passion is a gift for others that in turn provides her with satisfaction, fulfillment, and purpose in her life.

"To live a life of meaning we must engage ourselves in something meaningful."

Travel Log

Wanda, 78
Enthusiast About Making the World a Better Place

Wanda has a zest for life and great respect for the environment and the world around her. She says she inherited her passion for the great outdoors from her parents, both deceased, whom she described affectionately as "tree huggers."

"My parents enjoyed spending quality time outdoors and they passed their love of nature on to me," Wanda says.

Wanda's philanthropic nature and her commitment to family are demonstrated in her daily living. A widow for the past eight years, she honors the memory of her husband and her parents by treating all 18 members of her family to an annual seven-to-ten day trip to various parts of the United States. It's something she's been hosting for the past few years.

Imagine the family stories that will be retold for generations, the history lessons learned, and the photo albums that will be treasured for years to come. Wanda's passion and purpose in life comes, in part, by sharing her love of nature with the people she loves most – her family.

Travel Log

Mary, 56
Strong Emotion Around Literacy and Serving Seniors

Mary was a stay-at-home mom for more than 20 years and raised six children. Her family lived on a shoestring budget. Being resourceful, Mary pursued free programs and services in her community. Many hours were spent at the local library reading and checking out books. As a result, both Mary and her children developed a passion for reading. Mary enjoyed many delightful moments reading bedtime stories to her children.

Mary later went through a divorce and became a single parent. She was no stranger to having a limited income and, once again, needed to be creative and resourceful in finding money to manage the household and raise her children. She reflected on what she enjoyed most – reading and being outdoors.

Being clear regarding what she was passionate about allowed Mary to take advantage of two part-time jobs, one delivering library books to homebound seniors and helping with special programs aimed at seniors and another part-time job cleaning up and mowing a local park.

Continuing to pursue what she was passionate about, Mary eventually went on to receive a master's degree in library science. She now works in the foster grandparent program at her local Area Agency on Aging. Additionally, her experience at the agency prepared her for assisting her own parents when they needed nursing home care. Mary now has another passion: conducting research on the aging population. "I want to make the assisted living world just a little better than I found it. I have a great passion for my work and I'm very fulfilled."

If not now, when? Each of us have significant potential, yet few of us ever pursue it. Why? I believe the answer lies in the fact that we can do some things, but we cannot do everything. I have observed that many people allow someone else to determine what their potential is and how they spend their time. As a result, we may never slow down long enough to take time to look deep inside where our dreams lie and our passion and purpose are waiting to be discovered and fulfilled.

For others, the day to day "to dos" never end, leaving no time to pursue what is truly significant. Others, like the perfectionist, are their own worst enemy. They won't ever be able to get "it" right, whatever "it" is, so why try? Like the woman who never found the "right" time to have company over because her house was never quite "right."

For the procrastinator......well......they just never get around to making even a half-hearted try. Tomorrow always seems to be a better time to start.

Then there are still others who are waiting for a sign or some sort of change to take place in their lives before they will consider thinking about what their passion is and how to pursue it.

Reaching your potential requires focus. Ladies, when you embrace and pursue your personal passion, you will take a new look at what is really important to you and begin to prioritize everything you do from how you spend your time to how you spend your money. You will desire to live a more simplified, focused life. And the good news is your "to do" list will get shorter! Living intentionally makes decision making easier because nearly every endeavor will relate back to your purpose. In fact, it will redefine you as a highly capable woman on the *50&Forward* journey.

Identifying your passion may also help you discover the purpose for which the rest of your life is intended. When you know your purpose and are dedicated to reaching your maximum potential, you are well on your way to finding fulfillment.

Meaning comes through being intentional about your thoughts, words, and actions. When you find what you are passionate about, and intentionally commit to pursuing it, the rest will fall into place and life will indeed become more fulfilling and meaningful.

"Because of them I can now live the dream.
I am the seed of the free and I know it.
I intend to bear great fruits."

– Oprah Winfrey

Pursuing My Passion

Find a comfortable, quiet place without interruption and begin to discover your passion. Try to put aside all thoughts of the past and the future and <u>stay in the present</u>.

Side Trip #8 Directions

To get you started, I've provided four thought provoking questions designed to assist you in defining your passion. You may also want to look back at the travel logs in this chapter.

~ Do you have an **intense desire** deep in your soul?

~ Have you ever felt inspired or **enthusiastic** about using your gifts, talents or experiences to make the world a better place?

~ Have you overcome challenges that **inspire** you to give back to others?

~ Is there an **injustice** that sparks a **strong emotion in you**?

Defining My Passion

Based on your responses to the statements on page 146, make a list of what you are passionate about.

1.

2.

3.

4.

"A fulfilled woman is a possibility thinker. For her, each new day is a gift filled with unexpected delight."

– Oprah Winfrey

Finding your purpose in life will enable you to live more fully in the present while experiencing a sense of hope for the future. Creating a lifestyle that reduces your stress level will become a priority, allowing you to honor your physical, emotional, social, and spiritual health.

Purpose and fulfillment in life often have nothing to do with what you gain in life or accomplish for yourself. Instead, they are typically achieved when you focus on what you can do for others. Those around you will know what is important to you by how you spend your time and money. A woman who has a dream and lives her life intentionally, with passion and purpose, knows what she is willing to give up in order to live authentically. She will measure nearly everything she does according to whether or not it contributes to her purpose in life and the living, loving legacy she desires to develop and leave for others.

"If I had one wish for my children, it would be that each of them would reach for goals that would have meaning for them as individuals."

**– Lillian Carter,
mother of President Jimmy Carter**

My Life...

Points to Ponder...

Points to Ponder...

My Life...

Points to Ponder...

_____

_____

_____

_____

_____

_____

_____

_____

_____

_____

_____

_____

_____

_____

_____

_____

_____

_____

_____

_____

_____

My Legacy

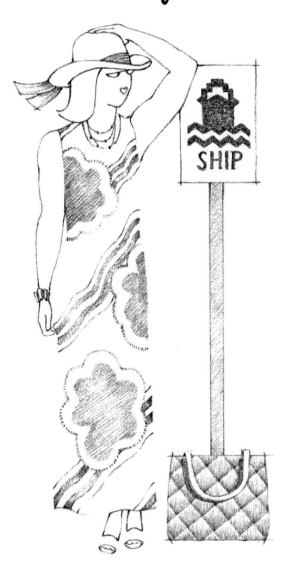

Legacy

~ **Financial**

~ **Physical**

~ **Emotional**

~ **Spiritual**

Values that are passed down from one generation to another.

Designing a Living, Loving Legacy

I am excited to have you traveling with me on this final leg of our journey as you begin to design your legacy.

Ladies, you are on a journey. As the "captain" of your own ship you have the opportunity to chart your own course. I invite you to reflect on the "Decades of Discovery" exercise beginning on page 88. Remember to borrow from valuable experiences and lessons you have learned through role models you most admire, both past and present. Their wisdom is a gift to you and to future generations. By acknowledging how their choices impacted your life financially, physically, emotionally, and spiritually, you will be better prepared to design and leave your own unique legacy.

You also have the option of choosing what "truths" you will pass down to future generations. I believe the single most valuable gift you can give yourself and your loved ones is the peace of mind that comes from being intentional and deliberate in creating your own unique and healthy living, loving legacy.

What is a legacy? Webster's defines "legacy" as something handed down from an ancestor or predecessor. While most people think of leaving their legacy in terms of money, it includes so much more. While working with women on the *50&Forward* journey, I began to notice a consistent pattern of thinking and observed that estate planning was more than planning for the end of our lives. Estate planning is comprehensive and includes planning to address both life and death issues surrounding one's financial, physical, emotional, and spiritual values.

This isn't your grandmother's estate planning. Gone are the days of the simple estate plan that consisted of a will explaining how your assets were to be distributed, and designating someone to carry out your wishes. Complicated tax and estate laws, and other legal issues, are largely to blame for muddying the waters regarding estate planning matters.

In addition, people are generally living longer. It's more likely than ever that you, or a family member, will become disabled, incapacitated, or face other health issues requiring long-term care.

I strongly believe that a more comprehensive estate plan is not only essential to protect your financial assets and physical well-being, it is also imperative to addressing your emotional and spiritual values, enabling you to design and leave a living, loving legacy.

A woman just beginning her **50&Forward** journey faces not only her own unique set of challenges, but also faces challenges so unique to her generation that few role models are available for guidance and direction. If this is you, the good news is you're not alone. You are warmly invited to join other women on this exciting new adventure of designing a unique, values-based estate plan.

Initially, many clients take a somber view of estate planning. They see it as simply "end of life" planning. Looked at from that perspective, it's no wonder many people would rather put it off as long as possible.

However, the new school of thought regarding estate planning emphasizes planning for the *rest* of your life. It advocates a balance between providing you with the means to pursue your goals and dreams, while simultaneously building and leaving a loving legacy that reflects your core values.

First, let's look at some of the legal terms involved in estate planning. While some of these terms may be unfamiliar to you or uncomfortable to think about, learning the basics will enable you to plan ahead and make wise choices that will have a lasting impact on your family and the organizations you hold most dear.

Keep in mind that laws vary from state to state. Depending on your specific situation an estate plan will include one or more of the following:

~ **Will:** A written document signed by you that explains your desires regarding how and to whom your property (assets) should be distributed upon your death.

~ **Revocable Trust:** A trust created during your lifetime into which assets are placed. You appoint a trustee, usually a trusted individual or a bank, who would invest and manage your assets on your behalf in the event of your death. Instructions from you regarding the management of the trust assets and the distribution of assets upon your death are included. "Revocable" means the trust can be changed or annulled at your discretion.

~ **Irrevocable Trust:** A trust that typically cannot be revoked, cancelled or changed after it is established. There are specific reasons why these types of trusts may be suitable given client objectives.

~ **Living Will:** Written directions from you regarding medical wishes in the event you are unable to speak for yourself. This document typically designates a patient advocate to make health care decisions on your behalf.

~ **Advance Directives:** This is an umbrella term that includes your living will and your designation of patient advocate.

~ **General Power of Attorney:** A legal designation given to the person you appoint to be responsible for managing your financial affairs and/or your health care affairs if you become unable to do so. Power of attorney can be given for all decisions or for health care decisions or financial decisions separately.

~ **Celebration of Life Plan (non-legal):** A detailed plan for your family to follow while organizing your end of life celebration. It should include elements that are significant and meaningful to you. Examples may include your favorite scriptures and songs, life sketch memories, favorite flowers, special photos, who you'd like to speak, and your preferred choices regarding memorial gifts. You may also want to consider incorporating components of your comprehensive values-based estate plan.

OK...enough mumbo jumbo!... In addition to these documents, I recommend a non-legal ethical will that relates the experiences you have had and the lessons you have learned to the values you uphold regarding the financial, physical, emotional, and spiritual components of your life. You may want to use this opportunity to share your most cherished or private experiences, world view, beliefs, and thoughts. Attached to your estate planning documents as an addendum, an ethical will is considered a separate document by most attorneys. Written by you, it should serve as an easy-to-read road map of your life that will hopefully bridge generations. It may even help future generations find their way in life.

Time to meet your flight crew. You are not alone on the **50&Forward** journey. Help is on the way! I want you to meet your qualified team of reputable professionals, standing by to help you put together your comprehensive estate plan.

Let's assemble your team:

~ CERTIFIED FINANCIAL PLANNER™ practitioner or other financial planning professional
~ Estate Planning Attorney
~ Accountant
~ Personal Historian

Certified Financial Planner™ practitioner (CFP®) or other trusted and knowledgeable financial professional. If chosen wisely, as discussed in the "My Money" section of this book, this professional is resourceful and has expertise to lead your team of estate planning professionals. An exceptional CFP® practitioner will:

~ **Help you compile** and **organize** your financial information by creating a list of your assets (house, vehicles, business interests, investments, retirement plans, insurance programs, liabilities, and more), ownerships, beneficiary designations, and prepare you for what information your attorney will need.
~ **Engage you in** a discussion regarding **what money means to you** and what your goals and dreams for the future include. A resourceful planner will make you aware of questions your attorney may ask, allowing you to think about your answers in advance. Many planners also assist you by **explaining** general concepts prior to meeting with your attorney

and are willing to further explain estate planning recommendations made by your attorney. This service often brings added peace of mind to a process that can seem overwhelming.

~ **Make** information **easily accessible** by providing you with a binder and organizing all **financial and legal documents** (financial statements, wills, trusts, powers of attorney, health care documents, copies of life insurance policies, health insurance policies, social security information, and any other valuable documents). In case of an emergency or untimely death, duplicate copies of this information can be stored in the advisor's office along with any delivery instructions provided by the client.

~ **Refer you** to reputable **attorneys**, **accountants**, **insurance providers**, and **bankers**. Some financial planners even go the extra mile by preparing and accompanying their clients to their initial consultation, or subsequent meetings, with other professionals. This will help protect you from being overwhelmed and provide added peace of mind.

~ **Discuss** any **tax consequences** associated with your estate and provide solutions regarding how to reduce estate and income taxes.

Estate planning attorney. Through experience and feedback from clients, a good estate planning attorney will:

~ **Listen, listen, listen**...they understand how overwhelming and emotionally charged this process can be!

~ **Provide feedback** to ensure they accurately heard your concerns, values, and wishes regarding quality of life and end of life issues.

~ **Ask critical questions** pertaining to your specific situation. They know the essential documents that need to be considered in an estate plan for married, widowed, divorced, and single women with or without children.

~ **Draft documents** for your review. These documents may include a will, living will, powers of attorney, a trust, pour-over will, guardianship, beneficiaries, patient advocates, and advance directives. The goal is to draft legal documents in accordance with your unique wishes and prevailing law.

~ **Discuss** any **tax consequences** associated with your estate and provide solutions regarding how to reduce estate taxes, allowing you to pass along a larger portion of your financial estate to your heirs.

~ **Review** your **financial documents** with your financial advisor and other professionals on your team, if requested.

~ They **understand** that **estate planning** is an evolving, ongoing process, and family dynamics and laws change over time. They will typically recommend you contact them every two to three years to review the terms of your estate planning documents.

Accountant. I typically recommend a Certified Public Accountant (CPA) due to the complexity of the tax laws involved in the financial and estate planning process. An experienced accountant will:

~ **Help you** understand how to **reduce your income taxes** so you can increase your net worth.

~ **Help you minimize estate taxes** in an effort to leave more to your loved ones and the organizations you hold dear.

~ **Keep you abreast of changes** that may impact your personal situation.

~ **Work with your financial advisor** to organize and coordinate your tax planning to ensure you are taking advantage of all applicable tax reduction strategies.

~ **Provide** you with a list of necessary paperwork in advance of **preparing** your annual tax return.

Personal Historian. A personal historian will:

~ **Help** you **organize** your thoughts regarding your emotional, spiritual, physical, and financial values and life lessons by asking meaningful questions to jog your memory and get your thoughts rolling.

~ **Listen, listen, listen** to your **story**, as you **reminisce**.

~ **Record** your **thoughts** and document your life story and life lessons using a tape recorder, video recorder or other media devices.

~ **Assist in selecting** the best **format** for telling your story (self-published book, PowerPoint, video production, photo journal, etc.).

~ **Creatively** design your project to ensure it is meaningful for future generations and represents your personality and unique journey.

Everyone has a story, but getting it down on paper to pass on to future generations may be a daunting task. The generations that come after you will treasure the autobiography of your life as they learn how their life is uniquely linked to yours. Some day your great-great-granddaughter may learn that her artistic talent, musical ability, knack for numbers, sense of humor, or red hair was something she inherited from you.

Perhaps it's time to be intentional about taking time to share your life's adventure with those you love. Children, even adult children, learn and remember best through stories. Open your heart and share both the humorous and perhaps difficult life experiences and lessons. Your loved ones will better understand you if they know how you have arrived at this point in your journey.

Remember, everyone has a story to share. If you don't tell yours, who will? Don't let this opportunity turn into "shoulda'," "coulda'," "woulda'." Do it now! Trust me, from all the stories I have heard, I know your loved ones will value hearing from you. Take heart if they don't seem to appreciate it now, they will later!

"I wish my mother had left me something about how she felt growing up. I wish my grandmother had done the same. I wanted my girls to know me."

– Carol Burnett

Creating a Comprehensive Values-Based Estate Plan

~ Financial

~ Physical

~ Emotional

~ Spiritual

I now invite you to thoughtfully consider each of these areas as you begin drafting your own comprehensive, values-based estate plan.

~ **Financial**
  ~ Your will and trust are legal documents that clearly dictate how your money is to be managed and designates who is to inherit your estate and when.
  ~ Your ethical will is a non-legal document you write. It clearly reflects your values, beliefs, and life lessons regarding earning, saving, investing, and spending money.

~ **Physical**
  ~ Your living will, a legal document, designates a patient advocate who will ensure your wishes regarding end of life issues are carried out.
  ~ The ethical will, a non-legal component, explains your personal thoughts regarding physical health, life lessons learned through your experiences with illness, and/or your thoughts regarding the importance of a balanced, healthy lifestyle.

~ **Emotional**
  ~ The ethical, non-legal will is a vehicle for sharing deepest thoughts and philosophies about life in general. It provides you with the chance to pass on the importance of character building traits like honesty, self-discipline, respect, appreciation, integrity, self-worth, forgiveness, and trust. It also provides an opportunity to express how important family and other loving relationships are. Specific core values, and how you came to adopt your value system, may also be included. Other important topics may include not taking things for granted, how to handle life's challenging or hurtful times, the importance of

education and lifelong learning and the ability to play and laugh.

~ **Spiritual**

    ~ The spiritual, non-legal will is a road map that marks the places where your life's dreams, passion, and purpose converge with the path you are on today. Landmarks will include your worldviews, your thoughts regarding forgiveness, the importance of traditions, faith, hope, dreams, and your moral code of conduct. It will allow your loved ones the privilege of understanding your story and assign to them the lessons you have learned by providing a clear, easy-to-read road map for them to follow.

Let's take a peek at examples in each category beginning with:

My Financial Legacy:

Too often beneficiaries don't have the slightest notion of how their benefactors earned, saved, invested and/or spent their money. If you are a woman on the *50&Forward* journey who has received an inheritance from a family member, you may find it important at some point to discover what kind of work and sacrifices your loved ones endured to help provide a future for them and you.

My own family heritage includes a great-grandfather, Harry, who was quite an entrepreneur as evidenced by his many business ventures. In particular, he founded the Berrien County Package Company in southwest Michigan. This company grew to be "one of the largest manufacturers of baskets in the fruit belt." Headlines I've read from the 1940s describe Harry as a "wealthy industrialist" and "a man who shunned publicity."

Regrettably, I know very little about his personal or professional life, except for the bits and pieces shared over family dinners and in old newspaper clippings.

The success of my ancestor's business ventures provided for a small financial legacy that will be passed down if managed wisely by generations before me. My hope and intent, should this happen, is to pass the legacy to my children, and their children, and their children's children. But because so much information has been lost, I often wonder what a financial inheritance will mean to future generations since there is such a big void for me.

I have absolutely no idea why my great-grandfather was driven to start this particular business or how it grew to be so successful. I wonder what his thoughts were relative to his own life and legacy. What were his parents and his own family like? What charities did he support? Was he involved in his community? Was he passionate and fulfilled? Was God a part of his life? What were his dreams? Did self-doubt ever creep in? What was it like having 170 employees harvest peaches on your farm in the 1940s?

I wonder what motivated this man. How I would cherish being able to sit down and talk with him and my other ancestors. What wisdom would they share with me? What life lessons would they pass on to me that I could pass on as well? What would they tell me about "money" - what it is and what it is not?

I can't recapture what has been lost. Recognizing the loss has motivated me to be intentional about my own legacy, both financial and otherwise, by creating written documentation allowing me to pass to future generations more than just the money I will leave behind.

If you can appreciate how hard your ancestors worked to accumulate their wealth, and realize the sacrifices they must have made, would you be inclined to spend your inheritance frivolously? If you could walk a mile in their shoes, would you spend the money wisely, or fritter it away "keepin' up with the Joneses?"

Perhaps you would be inclined to use the money to honor the values upheld by your family and, if possible, keep the family business going and growing, or launch a business of your own.

According to Thomas Stanley and William Danko, authors of *The Millionaire Next Door: The Surprising Secrets of America's Wealthy*, the assets most wealthy people have, if not inherited, came from living below their means, saving as much as possible, and earning one dollar at a time through motivation and hard work. In their book they cite a comment made by a company vice president following a banquet for ten first-generation millionaires:

"These people can't be millionaires! They don't dress like millionaires, they don't eat like millionaires, they don't act like millionaires – they don't even have millionaire names. Where are the millionaires who look like millionaires?"

Typically, people who actually earn their money are much more conservative in their spending habits than those who have inherited money free of sweat and toil.

As you begin to develop your financial values statement, consider the legacy you want to leave for future generations. Considering how money is being spent in today's "plastic" society, it would appear that younger generations are excessively vulnerable to accumulating debt at record levels with no thought of saving for a rainy day. "Instant gratification" is now the norm rather than the exception.

People often ask me questions like "who can afford to buy all these huge homes?" "How can my neighbors afford that boat, car, fancy vacation, etc.?" "How can people afford to buy second homes so freely?"

In the majority of cases, the truth is, their neighbors really *can't* afford all the "stuff." They're paying for it on credit and accumulating record levels of debt. They are following the "buy now, pay later plan," and like the man in a popular refinancing commercial says, "I'm in debt up to my eyeballs. Will somebody please help me?!" While this ad is funny and truthful, most ads are infuriating. "You're in debt? No problem. Keep spending and we'll help you spend more," the ads seem to suggest to vulnerable consumers who feel inferior if they aren't keepin' up with the Joneses.

According to a study published in the *Wall Street Journal*, Americans have become enormously dependent on borrowing against their homes to fuel their spending. Really, do we need an expensive study to tell us too many Americans are suffering from an affliction known as "Affluenza?" This phenomenon is described by economists John de Graaf and Vivian Boe in their PBS special, "Escape from Affluenza."

"Similar to the way flu germs are spread, rampant consumerism and materialism, spread by easy credit 'germs' are contaminating Americans of all colors and income levels and claiming more and more victims all the time."

– John and Vivian

The symptoms of "affluenza," according to de Graaf and Boe, include record levels of personal debt and bankruptcy, fractured families, chronic stress and overwork.

A new poll from the Center for a New American Dream reveals that 55 percent of Americans say they'd be willing to reduce material possessions and earnings either "some" or "a lot" in return for more time to spend with their families and less stress.

Additionally, 33 percent of us report buying 50 to 100 percent more "stuff" than we really need.

Ladies, there is a point here! If you are like most of my clients, you don't want to pass down a financial legacy that will fund or support a meaningless lifestyle that cannot be afforded by future generations.

"With expert advice and careful planning, you have the power to help stop 'affluenza' in its tracks. Leaving your values-based legacy and a road map for future generations will allow your loved ones to further understand what money means to you, what money is and what money is not. Doing so will plant seeds that make a difference."

– Jenna Everett

So, what exactly does money mean to you? How has your opinion regarding money changed over the years – the way it's earned, saved, spent, invested, gifted, etc.?

Studies of Americans born between 1965 and 1978, the so-called "Generation X" or "Xgen" (those currently between the ages of 29 and 42), indicate that most of them are willing to go into tremendous debt in pursuit of material possessions.

Along behind them come those born between 1979 and 1994, "Generation Y," or "Ygen" (those currently between the ages of 13 and 28). So intent are they to accumulate high-ticket items and expensive brand names. They are a marketing executive's dream come true!

Right behind them are the "tweens" (children currently around the ages of 9 and 14) who are being lavished with computers, cell phones, gaming systems, iPods, and other expensive toys to the tune of $1 billion and $2 billion per year, proving neither their parents nor grandparents have learned how to "just say no." After all, everyone has 'em, right?

> *"Parents and grandparents of the Xgen, Ygen, and tween generations are spending records levels of money "spoiling" these children and grandchildren. The sad fact is they are growing accustomed to it and now expect it."*
>
> **– Jenna Everett**

What's the point? How do you suppose the "Xgen," "Ygen," and "tween" generations would react to inheriting a substantial amount of money? After all, they rival their parents in purchasing clout.

To be fair, my husband and I have encountered beneficiaries who have received large inheritances and handled the money wisely. Unfortunately, we've also witnessed the reverse: beneficiaries spending tens and even hundreds of thousands of dollars over the span of a few years on what you and I would consider frivolous, meaningless things.

> *"People buy things they don't need, with money they don't even have, to impress people they don't even like."*

If you need expensive things to make up for something lacking in your life, such as love, respect, success, purpose, meaning, self-worth, etc., there's not enough money in the world to make you happy. Spending so frivolously will dishonor the memory of your benefactors and defeat their wishes and desires. Let's be clear: money will not make you happy. Money can, however, bring joy when it is spent on meaningful, values-based decisions.

I hope the following examples will get you thinking about your own financial affairs and encourage you to be intentional and deliberate about your financial legacy.

Travel Log | **Jerry, 43, Jackie, 45**
Nest Egg Gets Cracked and Fried

As professionals earning six figures between them, Jerry and Jackie were already enjoying a standard of living most Americans can only dream about. Then they inherited $600,000.

We took them through the process of comprehensive financial planning, first allocating appropriate dollars to help educate their four children. Next, we helped them set up a retirement fund and allocated money for a trip overseas. Additionally, we set aside $100,000 for "play money."

The idea was to create a comfortable nest egg so Jerry and Jackie could do something great with it one day. Unfortunately a plan is only as good as its execution.

It didn't take long for them to treat the $100,000 they'd set aside literally like "play money," after which they began whittling away at the remainder of their inheritance. Over the course of seven years, they'd spent every penny. And sadly, they had very little to show for it.

It makes one wonder what values regarding money Jerry and Jackie had learned. It also caused me to wonder what kind of role modeling they saw demonstrated growing up and if a values-based financial statement regarding money would have assisted in heading off Jackie and Jerry's disaster.

Instead, the quality of this couple's lives, and the impact their choices have had on their children's futures, has been devastating. Quite possibly, the money they inherited did them more damage than good.

Lydia, 23
Seventy Year-Old Grandparents Meant Well

Lydia was a part-time college student when she inherited over $200,000 from her grandparents' estate. Because she lacked the maturity to see beyond the present and didn't choose to listen to loved ones or expert financial counsel, she dropped out of school, bought a hot red sports car and began living off her inheritance.

Her party lifestyle led to experimenting with drugs, which eventually landed her in jail. Too late, Lydia now realizes it would have been beneficial if her grandparents had provided her with some insight regarding their values about money and what benefits they hoped Lydia would receive. Adding a provision stating the money was to be used for college first, after which only a "sprinkling" of money would become available to her each year, along with other boundaries and limits, may have been helpful as well.

Travel Log | Carol, 51, Joe, 51
Windfall Wise

Raising three children is expensive! Carol worked at home while the children were growing up. Even though Joe had a middle management position with a large firm, expenses for braces, summer camps, and college tuition, etc., caused the couple to take a very conservative approach to spending unnecessarily.

As their third child approached college age, Joe unexpectedly received a fairly sizeable inheritance. They used some of the money to help their two oldest children pay off their college debts and invested the rest to help pay for upcoming college expenses and build a nest egg for their retirement.

Joe and Carol then talked with their children about contributing some of the money to charity, and as a family they chose one everyone felt passionate about.

How fortunate Joe and Carol's children were to experience their parents' wise use of a windfall. By sharing and role modeling the importance of their financial and life values, they provided their children with the opportunity to observe and experience the importance of making wise and healthy choices with money. The lessons learned will no doubt serve them well for many years to come.

All that glitters...

If you've ever watched the "Antiques Road Show," or other similar programs, you've seen people bring in "Great-Aunt Betty's tea service" or "Grandpa's old baseball cards" for appraisal. Money isn't the only commodity passed on to future generations. A typical inheritance could include the valuable treasures you hold most dear including crystal, collections, figurines, jewelry, paintings, sculptures, china, and antique furniture to name a few. I placed these material items in the financial section because whether kept or sold, they all qualify as assets.

Sad but true, it appears these treasures are of little value to future generations. It is my belief, however, that if those inheriting your treasures knew the significance and emotional value they held, your heirs' choice to sell them to the highest bidder would be different. I invite you to consider including directions in your will regarding who you would like to receive your valuable or sentimental possessions. Additionally, I encourage you to include within your financial values statement the significance of these possessions and the story behind them.

Financial Legacy Focus

Within your estate planning document, consider including a *financial values statement* that explains what money means to you – what it is and what it isn't. Consider writing down your thoughts and experiences and share them with your loved ones while you are living. This will help them understand your values and viewpoints.

Side Trip #9 Directions

It's time to grab a piece of paper and pencil once again. Find a quiet place for reflection. Begin thinking about your financial life experiences and the life lessons you would like to share regarding earning, saving, investing, and spending money. I have included the following questions to help you think about what to include in your *Financial Values Statement* for future generations to know and understand.

1. Look back at the "My Money" section. What lessons did you learn during your formative years about earning, saving, investing and spending money?

2. What was your first meaningful experience with money?

3. What was your first job?

4. Did you save your money for something special?

5. Do you remember your first investment or savings account?

6. Did you attend college or other form of continued learning? If so, who paid your tuition and other expenses?

7. Consider your adult life. What choices did you make regarding earning, saving, investing, and spending money?

8. When, and for what, did you first use a credit card?

9. Describe your first car. Your first house. Did someone help you with the down payment? How did you pay for it?

10. What good choices did you make and why?

11. What poor choices did you make? What did you learn?

12. What expenditure has brought you the most joy? Why?

13. Think about who will inherit your money and your treasured possessions. Are there stories or lessons you need to share that will promote the continuation of your financial values and preserve your financial legacy?

Example: Dee, 65

Dee grew up in a large five-bedroom country home, originally owned by her grandfather, five miles outside the city of St. Clair, Michigan. Dee's father worked hard tending to the family dairy farm. Their rural home had only one small bathroom and a cistern for water. Imagine growing up with nine siblings and one bathroom!

Dee was no stranger to hard work at an early age. One of her happiest memories was of her father taking freshly harvested wheat to the "elevator" to be cut into grain. Dee will always remember how excited she and her sisters felt on those crisp fall days when Daddy's green 1949 GMC pick-up truck pulled in the driveway. The pick-up was loaded with an array of pretty patterned cotton sacks filled with freshly cut grain. As soon as Daddy pulled up, Dee and her sisters would shout, "Here comes the grain, let's pick out our favorite colored patterns!" Their mother would proudly make dresses out of the girls' favorite handpicked grain sacks. Dee considers this experience to be one of her fondest memories – it was a real family celebration.

Dee will never forget the many times she and her family traveled to Aunt Hilda and Uncle Bill's house on Christmas holidays. Even though their home was only five miles away, going to the "city" was exciting for Dee. She loved spending time with her cousins, including her "favorite" cousin Janet, playing dolls and paper dolls.

On one particular Christmas, when Dee was seven, it was time to exchange gifts. Everyone gathered around the Christmas tree. One of the family's favorite traditions was for each person to open his or her gifts one at a time and carefully pass them around for all to see. With all the excitement, Aunt Hilda thought it would be a good idea to keep things organized. She set out a large sewing machine size-box for each of her three daughters to place their unwrapped treasures in. Dee's mother commented, "What a nice way to keep things organized." Without thinking, Dee blurted out, "All _we_ would need is a small shoebox to place all our gifts in."

All was quiet during the ride home. Later that evening, one of Dee's older sisters sat her down for a heart to heart talk and lovingly said, "Do you have any idea what our parents had to sacrifice to save enough money to buy our Christmas gifts? I know you didn't mean to hurt Mom and Dad's feelings, but do you realize how your comment about the shoebox made them feel?"

Values-based lessons Dee learned:
- ~ While visiting my aunt and uncle at Christmas, I made my first connection between "money and buying things" at the age of seven.
- ~ My parents gave up a lot and worked hard to provide my nine siblings and me with the necessities.
- ~ Being frugal means not being wasteful or spending money freely or unnecessarily.
- ~ In high school and college, I remember challenging myself to see how far I could stretch a dollar. It felt really good!
- ~ I learned not to take the little things for granted.
- ~ Life is uncertain. Be prepared for the unexpected by setting aside money.
- ~ Money is security and provides peace of mind.
- ~ Money does not buy happiness.

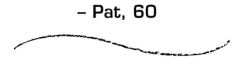

"It is important to take care of our physical bodies. After all, our bodies house our heart and our spirit, our mental and emotional being."

– Pat, 60

My Physical Legacy:

Have you ever considered how your daily routine and commitment to physical health, or lack thereof, may be the direct result of what was modeled or not modeled to you in your early years and how these choices can leave a lasting impression on future generations?

Have you considered the importance of knowing your family's medical history and the benefits of passing it on? Sharing this valuable information with your loved ones may save a life or improve the longevity and/or quality of their life. Think of the woman who learns she has a history of heart disease in her family. Having this valuable information may allow her to take preventative steps now to increase longevity and quality of life later. It also provides a lasting road map for loved ones to follow.

Perhaps you or a loved one has struggled with an illness or health problem. How do you physically and mentally cope with life's physical challenges? What impact does the power of positive attitude and spirituality have on health?

Maybe you always wanted to be more physically active but never had a role model to follow. It's not too late to change that. In fact, it will not only benefit you, it will also provide a much needed positive role model for young people fighting childhood obesity. Consider the fun you could have swimming, hiking, golfing, playing tennis, bowling or even skiing.

In your ethical, non-legal will, share your personal thoughts regarding the importance of physical health and the life lessons you've learned through your experiences with illness, and/or your thoughts regarding the importance of focusing on a balanced, productive, and healthy lifestyle.

Travel Log

Judy, 59
Body Image Impacts Quality of Life

Throughout junior high and high school Judy felt insecure, insignificant, unloved, and ashamed because, "in my head I felt I was fat and unacceptable."

These feelings of inadequacy contributed to an eating disorder that took a physical toll on Judy's body. Eventually, observant, caring friends and family members convinced her to seek professional guidance.

Today, after several years of abusing her body, Judy has regained control of her life and sees herself in a positive, constructive light.

"It's been a long, hard journey for me, but I've been blessed with loving memories of all the people who tried to help me. They cared so deeply for me, but I didn't see it that way for a long time. My struggle and my challenge is something I've only shared with a few people. The lessons I have learned from my situation are the legacy I can pass to other young girls fighting the same illness. I hope to have a positive impact on their lives and convince them that they are unconditionally loved just as I was."

Physical Legacy Focus

It's time to get out paper and pencil once again. Find a quiet place that's conducive to reflection and begin pondering your physical life experiences and the lessons you have learned regarding health. I've included the following questions to help you begin drafting your **physical values statement** for future generations to know and understand.

Side Trip #10 Directions

You may want to turn back to the completed "Decades of Discovery" beginning on page 93 to get you started.

1. While growing up, how did you feel about your body?

2. Did you have a healthy self-image?

3. What healthy lifestyle habits did you see modeled while growing up? Consider the following: dietary choices, sleep habits, benefits of regular exercise, use of prescription and other drugs, use of alcohol and tobacco, impact of attitude on health, etc.

4. Did your family eat meals together?

5. What physical activities or sports did you participate in as a child?

6. Did anyone teach you recreational sports like skiing, bowling, tennis, racquetball, hiking, swimming, running, walking, biking or golf?

7. Did your family exercise together?

8. If anyone, who did you learn your healthy lifestyle choices from?

9. What healthy habits have you developed regarding the topics in #3?

10. What healthy habits will you choose to pass on to future generations?

11. Are you modeling what is important to you?

12. What are your thoughts regarding the aging process?

13. Do you know your family's medical history? What is it?

Example: Linda, 67

For many years Linda was addicted to tobacco and became dependant on alcohol. What started as "social drinking" escalated. Eventually, her life became totally unmanageable and she no longer had the ability to stop after the first drink.

Linda's family recognized she had a serious problem and took action by admitting her to a hospital for alcoholism. It was there that for the first time she realized, and admitted, she was an alcoholic. Linda is forever grateful to her family and the Alcoholics Anonymous program. She continues to attend AA meetings and works at living her life by the twelve steps of the AA program. It's been 32 years now since Linda gave up drinking. It's been 27 years since Linda gave up smoking. She decided to replace these addictions with a healthy lifestyle that includes exercising several days a week. And what a commitment...she's been consistent all these years. Additionally, Linda decided to take up race walking and has competed in many race walking events. Today her wall is decorated with all of her ribbons and medals for her children and grandchildren to enjoy. What an inspiration!!!

Linda is leaving a legacy of overcoming addictions and an attitude that demonstrates "nothing is impossible," "I CAN do it," and, "I choose to lead an active, healthy lifestyle."

In addition, Linda has been able to warn her older grandchildren about a tendency toward alcoholism on both sides of their family and the personal risks they may face if they choose to start drinking.

Linda is intentional and deliberate about talking openly with her children and grandchildren. She is choosing to take the time to talk candidly with her loved ones. Currently she is working with a personal historian to record her life story.

Values-based lessons Linda learned:

~ It is possible to overcome an alcohol addiction if you acknowledge that you have a problem. I realized alcohol was controlling my life and if I didn't stop, it would eventually kill me.

~ I realize the importance of being open and honest with my children and grandchildren about the history of alcoholism in our family.

~ I will be intentional and deliberate about helping future generations understand the warning signs and devastating effects of drinking.

~ Physical exercise is good for the mind, body, and spirit.

~ Physical exercise reduces stress and the desire for unhealthy vices.

~ Being involved in physical activity with a group of like-minded people is exhilarating.

~ We should never take our health for granted.

~ It's up to us to be mindful of taking care of ourselves.

~ I hope to demonstrate for many more years the benefits of healthy living.

~ I plan to engage my grandkids in talking about making healthy choices.

~ I know the importance of leaving my medical history for my family.

My Emotional Legacy:

In discussions with so many women, I realized what a profound impact our words and actions have on others. Children, including adult children, are like video cameras in that they are recording, watching, replaying, and reacting to what others do and say.

Leaving a clear, easy to read emotional road map will assist in building a healthy self-image and boost the self-esteem and confidence of those you love.

Your commitment to modeling and discussing the importance of character building traits is critical to family values and developing an honorable moral code of conduct. Values like honesty, respect, appreciation, hard work, self-discipline, integrity, self-worth, forgiveness, thoughtfulness, and trust can be passed on. Additionally, it provides an opportunity to express how important family and other loving relationships are, including appropriately expressing feelings during life's challenges or hurtful times, not taking things for granted, the importance of education and lifelong learning, and the ability to play and laugh.

For example, when you teach others the foolishness of holding grudges, and instead choose to demonstrate forgiveness, you teach your loved ones the liberating power of "living with forgiving." Or perhaps you demonstrate the power of peace, solitude, and the voice of quiet reason, a gift in today's fast-paced world. Or maybe you have maintained the lost art of letter writing. Just think how delighted the recipients will be to receive a hand-written note in their mailboxes. Your thoughtfulness demonstrates the time and care you spent on their behalf.

"It's by spending one's self that one becomes rich."

– Sarah Bernhardt

One of my favorite joy-filled childhood memories is running through the pouring rain without a care in the world, laughing at myself and how drenched I got. It felt SO good, so refreshing. It made me feel alive! Today, just the smell of fresh rainfall takes me back to those wonderful times.

Ironically, 30 years later, one of my favorite memories with my husband and our three sons, Ryan, Austin, and Lane, is spontaneously stopping along the riverside during a sudden, unexpected downpour. There was no lightning to keep us from running, dancing, laughing, and singing as clusters of car passengers wrenched their necks to catch a glimpse of us EXPERIENCING life. To top off our delight, we were blessed with the most gorgeous rainbow.

Why is it most of us no longer feel comfortable enjoying the kinds of random, silly acts that were second nature to us when we were young? Why do we become increasingly inhibited as we age? My hope, my passion, my desire is that thirty years from now, I will be splashing around in a mud puddle with my grandchildren, soaked to the skin and as happy as I was way back when.

While others may think of these actions as silly and meaningless, they represent a valuable lesson I wish to leave for my family and loved ones: the simple pleasures of childhood can continue to bring us joy throughout our lives.

And isn't it funny how many of the experiences that bring us the greatest joy in life don't cost a penny?

Many of the things that brought me joy as a child will continue to bring me joy throughout the rest of my life. I will smile when I recall our time in that downpour, teaching our children the half-remembered words to "Singin' in the Rain." The truth I hope to teach them is that being spontaneous and flexible will bring unexpected joy and laughter throughout their lives, something, at times, I have to relearn myself.

> *"I know that my actions and how I spend my time and my money show my children and others what is important to me. I can say what is important but they will know what is important by the way I live my daily life."*
>
> **– Jenna Everett**

I also have many fond memories surrounding the beauty of holiday celebrations. (Though the thought of my mother "passing the baton" to me seems a bit overwhelming!)

Those tantalizing aromas coming from the kitchen have always created fond memories for everyone. I remember exclaiming, "I can't wait to eat." Now my children share the same sentiment.

I have to admit (and shame on me) that there were years, particularly when my children were younger, when the thought of me keeping this tradition alive seemed unmanageable. I'd grumble to my mother, "Why do we go through all this hassle?" She would just smile.

Imagining my turn as hostess and thinking about all that shopping, baking, peeling, cutting, sautéing, boiling, mashing, stuffing, and simmering was enough in itself to wear me out.

And dare I mention the work involved in setting the table with my great-grandmother's Royal Doulton china, polishing my grandmother's sterling silver (accumulated piece-by-piece when she was a young woman working at the local jewelry store), and shining up her crystal? The table is always stunningly beautiful and elegant, making everyone feel like royalty...but what an undertaking!

In recent years it has dawned on me – it's all about tradition and legacy. My children look forward to the holidays and our special family time around the table. This past year we each chose a family member's name out of a crystal bowl and took the time to tell a memorable story about that person and share an attribute we appreciated most about them. Like most families, it can sometimes be "challenging" to find kind words to say; nevertheless, it's the kind of exercise that teaches us to find the good in everyone.

Even the "cool" teenagers look forward to Grandma's mashed potatoes and dressing, stuffing themselves with turkey, and partaking in conversation, games, and cards as we laugh and reminisce together. We all anticipate the pumpkin pie with loads of fresh whipped cream, which comes later in the day after our faces hurt from laughing.

These are the times that bond our families and reinforce the values we uphold. I get it now! My mother is building a lasting legacy of love, devotion, and commitment for her children and grandchildren. Family, togetherness and making our times together special are her passion. Like my mother, grandmother, and great-grandmother, I hope to carry on this valued tradition of preparing and serving formal holiday meals.

"We can do no great things, only small things with great love."

– Mother Theresa

Travel Log

Pat, 60
Making the Time for Memories

Pat has fond memories of the times she spent at her grandparents' home.

"My grandma made the best cookies and pies and the house always smelled wonderful. I felt good every time I visited," she says.

Pat recalls her grandparents always taking time to ride their bikes with her. At night, they would build a bonfire and the family would gather around to talk or tell stories.

Visits were always filled with crafts, catching frogs and letting them go, snuggling up against a soft arm at night, and being read to or watching a movie, the endings of which she often couldn't remember the next day when she found herself mysteriously waking up in her mother's old bedroom.

"I always felt special when I visited there, like I was the most important person in the world to them," Pat said, adding that she hopes to make time for the special little things – leaving her own grandchildren with a legacy similar to the one her grandparents left for her.

My Legacy...
Side Trip #11

Emotional Legacy Focus

It's time to get out paper and pencil once again. Find that quiet place for reflection and begin thinking about your emotional life experiences and lessons you've learned regarding emotional health. I've included the following questions to help you begin thinking about what to include in your **emotional values statement** for future generations to know and understand.

Side Trip #11 Directions

As you review the suggested questions for writing your emotional legacy, you may discover you did not have a good role model. The good news is you have the opportunity to rewrite your story by being intentional and deliberate about modeling and telling your loved ones about the importance of having a healthy, balanced emotional life.

You may want to turn back to the completed "Decades of Discovery" beginning on page 93 to get you started.

1. What values did you see modeled and what lessons did you learn about honesty, respect, loyalty, appreciation, trust, hard work, integrity, self-worth, forgiveness, generosity, thoughtfulness, etc.?

2. Did someone mentor and/or support you?

3. Who is most dear to your heart and why?

4. Who made you feel special and why?

5. Think of the times you felt most content as a child. Where were you? Who was involved? What were you doing?

6. What are your fondest childhood memories? Why?

7. How did you learn to handle mistakes?

8. How did you handle loss or the death of a loved one?

9. How did you make it through tough, hurtful times?

10. Who taught you about feelings and how to appropriately express them during times of sadness, anger, and hurt?

11. Did someone teach you the importance of education, lifelong learning, and the ability to play and laugh?

12. Are you modeling what is important to you?

13. Consider the first 11 questions. Are you living and leaving a legacy of emotional health for those you love?

Example: Marjorie, 61

Marjorie grew up observing her parents working well as a team in the family business. Life was good for Marjorie both at home and in school. Marjorie knew she was deeply loved by her family.

Marjorie recalls living in an above average home, attending Catholic boarding school and dating the "big man on campus," a boy who had been a football star in their hometown of Gary, Indiana.

They stopped seeing each other after three years, but during his visit home from the military, Marjorie became pregnant as a result of a "fling." It was a socially shameful situation for both Marjorie and her parents. A good little Catholic girl from an upstanding family becoming pregnant out-of-wedlock was unthinkable.

The decision was made by her parents that Marjorie would take up residence with a family, in their home, through Catholic Charities in Chicago where her pregnancy would remain a secret. Marjorie's parents never saw the cold cinderblock basement where Marjorie stayed for the duration of her pregnancy. In exchange for her accommodations, Marjorie was required to babysit the five children who lived in the home, cook, and clean. The money Marjorie earned was then used toward her baby's delivery. Through it all Marjorie remained in a state of denial that she describes as a kind of "out of body experience."

On December 23, 1965, at the age of 19, Marjorie gave birth to a beautiful little girl who was immediately whisked away from her and put up for adoption. For 37 years Marjorie locked away her little secret and the shame it brought in the deepest corner of her heart.

In 2001 her mother passed away and it was during this time of brokenness that Marjorie realized how important it was to forgive herself and reconcile her past with her present.

"My mother's death made me realize how much I had lost and I felt I needed to come to terms with my past."

A year later, Marjorie decided to quietly pursue the whereabouts of her now 37-year-old daughter.

"The goal was not necessarily to meet my daughter but to provide her with information about her biological family and medical history. I prayed 'dear God, whatever happens, help me accept it,'" she said.

Through a series of nothing short of miraculous events (the adoption records were kept closed and confidential) Marjorie not only located her daughter, Cathy, but discovered her daughter had been searching for her during the same period of time.

Today, Marjorie and her husband share the blessings of a beautiful daughter, a son-in-law, and three adorable grandchildren. Cathy is blessed with two wonderful mothers she lovingly refers to as "mom" and "mommy." Her adoptive father, who passed away 12 years ago, would be happy to know Cathy has had the gift of two great fathers.

"I learned that out of nearly every bad situation comes something good and being authentic and real frees your body and soul. It's about trust and faith," Marjorie said, adding, "It never occurred to me that my daughter would love me."

Values-based lessons Marjorie learned:

~ Feeling shame is not healthy or productive.

~ No one is perfect. We all make mistakes.

~ Holding grudges weighs you down.

~ A mistake can be our worst mistake or our best mistake.

~ God can make something beautiful out of our brokenness.

~ Out of brokenness comes truth.

~ Forgive yourself, and others, and let go of the past.

~ Sometimes what we think is bad isn't really so bad.

~ Life is all about trust and faith.

~ People can get along well when they don't have baggage.

~ If you get a second chance, take it.

~ I'm on the back nine and I need to make it count.

~ It's time to give back to those I love.

~ My hopes and dreams lie in my family.

My Spiritual Legacy

In writing content for the "spiritual legacy" section, it became clear our spiritual and emotional legacy components are many times inseparable, especially those involving forgiveness, family values, moral code of conduct, etc.

Your spiritual legacy marks the places where your life's dreams, passions, and purpose converse with the path you are on today. Landmarks will include your worldview, your thoughts regarding forgiveness and family values and the importance of tradition, faith, hopes and dreams. Leaving your spiritual legacy provides those you love the privilege of understanding how acknowledging, honoring and living your dreams, passion, and purpose bring true, lasting fulfillment.

And, in a world that seems increasingly morally neutral, perhaps your unswayable moral compass will provide a strong foundation for your loved ones to cling to. Your spiritual legacy will also clarify your beliefs about why you were placed on this earth and how you can leave your little corner of the world a bit better than you found it.

"When we pour ourselves into our passions, into what is important to us, we make a difference for others and we are simultaneously offered the opportunity to experience real fulfillment and joy."

Evie, 48
Honesty Always the Best Path

Evie's mother Ruth worked at a manufacturing company where she labored cutting rubber to fit around automobile headlights. Evie recalls the time her mother lost the diamond out of her wedding ring while at work. Even at a young age, Evie could sense her mother's deep disappointment and sadness over her loss.

Ruth immediately called their insurance agent to inform him of the loss of the diamond out of her setting. He responded by saying, "Don't tell me you've lost just your diamond, tell me you've lost your whole ring."

He then explained to Ruth that her whole ring was insured, but not just the diamond alone, and proceeded to suggest that she restate her claim.

Honesty was an important value to Ruth and she refused to take the agent's advice even though it meant not recovering insurance money to replace her lost diamond. It simply was not part of Ruth's value system to be dishonest. Ruth's **words and actions** demonstrated what was important to her. This decision left a very deep and lasting impact on young, impressionable Evie.

Thankfully, when Ruth returned to work the next day, she lifted a huge piece of rubber off the ground and, to her surprise, she spotted her gleaming diamond stuck to it. Ruth often joked that she found a diamond in the rough that day. She was so grateful.

"My mom is my hero. She showed me that honesty is always the best path to take," Evie said. "Of course, honesty may not always reward you with a lost treasure, but for the sake of your self-esteem, it's always the best path to take. When we choose to act dishonestly, it hardens our hearts."

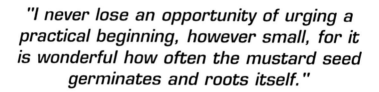

"I never lose an opportunity of urging a practical beginning, however small, for it is wonderful how often the mustard seed germinates and roots itself."

– Florence Nightingale

Spiritual Legacy Focus

It's time to get out paper and pencil once again. Find that quiet place for reflection and begin thinking about your spiritual life experiences and lessons you've learned regarding spiritual health. I've included the following questions to help you begin thinking about what to include in your **spiritual values statement** for future generations to know and understand.

Side Trip #12 Directions

Like many women I've talked with, you may struggle with an artificial belief that your legacy isn't really that important because you feel you have no special gifts or talents or experiences worth mentioning. Rest assured, my friend, it's in life's little contributions, especially those surrounding your dreams, passion, and purpose that will bring real and lasting fulfillment and will provide a spiritual compass, a guide, a foundation for yourself and for those you love.

Because there is a strong connection between your past, the present, and the spiritual legacy you will develop and leave, you may want to reread the "My Life" section of this book, located on pages 82–151, before proceeding with this side trip exercise.

1. Look back at the "My Life" section of the book. What was your experience as a child with faith and hope?

2. Was God a part of your life growing up? If so, what spiritual truths did you learn?

3. Who modeled spiritual truths to you? What was their impact on you?

4. Whose words and actions positively impacted you as a child?

5. Did someone inspire you because of his or her enthusiasm or aspirations?

6. When was the first time you shared a goal or a hope for the future with someone? How did they respond?

7. Were you enthusiastic as a young person? Why?

8. Consider your adult life. What choices have you made regarding spirituality, dreams, and fulfillment?

9. How did you develop your worldview? What is it based on?

10. Is the Bible relevant in your daily life? Why?

11. What is your moral code of conduct? Are you living and verbalizing what you believe?

12. Do you believe in absolute truth?

13. What spiritual choices do you believe have been healthy? Why?

14. What poor spiritual choices have you made? What did you learn?

15. What brings you joy in daily living?

16. What is the purpose of your life? Are you living it?

17. What spiritual truths do you hope to pass on?

18. What are your thoughts regarding heaven and eternity?

Example: Helen, 58

Helen had come to a crossroads in her life. "Work was crazy and I felt overwhelmed and unfulfilled. I was on the 'treadmill of life' going nowhere fast," Helen said. She knew in her heart it was time for a change. "Trusting God had a plan, I took time to be still and reflect on my life." During her moments of quiet reflection, Helen began to reminisce and recall all the kind, meaningful words friends and family had shared with her through the years including, "You're such a good hostess," "You're so comfortable to be with and a great listener," "Your timing is always perfect, you just seem to know when I need a word of encouragement," and "You have the gift of organization, you make it look so easy."

Helen never gave much thought to these comments and the impact her words and actions had on those around her. Seeking clear direction, Helen prayed that God would help her see what He wanted to do through her seemingly ordinary life. "I'm a simple person and I've always had a passion for serving others. I guess you could say I've always dreamed of having more time to support, encourage and give back." Little did Helen know her "small" insignificant dream would lead her to discover the purpose for which her life was intended and also provide her with the greatest sense of peace and fulfillment she had ever known.

"I thank God for stirring my spirit and slowing me down," Helen shared. Over the past few years Helen's journey has been focused on helping others experience God's love, peace and joy. She has also served as a missionary both domestically and abroad. With a big grin on her face and her hands raised in the air Helen stated, "The more I focus on God's plan, and on others, the more blessed I feel."

Values-based lessons Helen learned:

~ Dreams + Passion + Purpose = Real and Lasting Fulfillment.
~ The time to live dreams is now.
~ Allow others to share in your dreams – it will inspire you
~ Identifying your passion will help you discover the purpose for which your life was intended.
~ When someone tells you you're good at something, take heart and listen.
~ Understanding your purpose helps prioritize life.
~ Living intentionally makes decision making simpler; every decision directly relates back to your purpose.
~ *"Be still and know that I am God."* Psalms 46:10. Taking time to be quiet is essential to living a purpose filled, meaningful, balanced life.
~ I am clay in the potter's hand.
~ Life is about unconditionally loving others.

So, ladies, what are you waiting for? I encourage you to set aside time to ponder, share and record your thoughts, values, and life lessons regarding your financial, physical, emotional and spiritual journey. If you've taken time to complete most of the side trips covered on the previous pages, your life experiences and lessons will be fresh in your mind. I also encourage you to record your journey in writing – what a gift to those you love.

My Legacy...

Points to Ponder...

My Legacy...

Points to Ponder...

_____

_____

_____

_____

_____

_____

_____

_____

_____

_____

_____

_____

_____

_____

_____

_____

_____

_____

_____

My Legacy…

Points to Ponder…

_____

_____

_____

_____

_____

_____

_____

_____

_____

_____

_____

_____

_____

_____

_____

_____

_____

_____

Packing with a Purpose

My Life...

My Money...

My Legacy...

During your journey through this book, I've shared with you the importance of being intentional and deliberate regarding what to carry forward. Ladies, no more "side trips"...it's time to pack for your authentic **50&Forward®** journey.

Remember, the goal is to lighten your load and begin "Packing with a Purpose." Just think how much easier your journey will be without excess baggage. Check your bags. How much carry on luggage do you have? This is your life and it's up to you to choose what is important to you. Remember to pack your financial, physical, emotional, and spiritual life lessons and values.

For your convenience, I have provided you with "My Money," "My Life," and "My Legacy" bags on pages 218–220. Please take time to write down what you would like to pack and what is better left behind.

See you at our "Final Boarding Call!"

"My Money" Bag

I'm packing:

_____

_____

_____

_____

_____

_____

_____

_____

_____

"My Life" Bag

I'm packing:

"My Legacy" Bag

I'm packing:

_____

_____

_____

_____

_____

_____

_____

_____

Final Boarding Call

My Money…

My Life…

My Legacy…

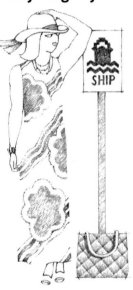

Whew! Glad you're still with me. No time to waste. Ladies, it's time for your *50&Forward®* journey!

As you prepare for your journey, please take a moment to reflect on how far you've come and the many lessons you've learned. On the first leg of your journey, you discovered that having your financial affairs in order can bring peace of mind. You also explored what matters most and the benefits of hiring a CERTIFIED FINANCIAL PLANNER™ practitioner to assist you. However, it's not just about money matters; it's about other things that matter.

On your journey through the "My Life" and "My Legacy" sections of the book you learned about the importance of building a secure future for your loved ones and a healthy productive lifestyle that's balanced for yourself – financially, physically, spiritually, and emotionally.

I am convinced that throughout life we either move forward or we go backwards – there is no in between. You were designed for a purpose with a dream in your heart and you are among many wonderful women who have weathered life's ups and downs and have gracefully arrived at midlife wiser and more radiant than ever.

Now, more than ever, women *50&Forward®* are choosing to travel with passion and purpose. They are choosing to take only the items that will add value to their purpose in life and the legacy they desire to leave behind. I invite you to pack with the same purpose in mind.

Ladies, I hope this book has been helpful in allowing you to catch a glimpse of the exciting possibilities that await you. My heartfelt desire is that you will choose to be intentional and deliberate about living your life with passion and purpose.

The next phase of your "real life" ***50&Forward®*** journey is just beginning. The "someday" you've been waiting for is here. You've withstood the test of time and now it's *your* time. Come along, let's pack our bags – there's not a moment to lose!

All Aboard!

Whether you received this book directly from *50&Forward*®, borrowed it from a friend, received it as a gift, or purchased it for yourself at a bookstore, it is our hope that your journey through its pages proved meaningful and empowering!

Please let us know what you have discovered or experienced on your unique journey. We would be delighted to hear from you.

For more information regarding book orders, speaking engagements or seminars we invite you to contact us:

E-mail:
50andForward@sbcglobal.net

Toll Free:
877-983-7707

Address:
2603 Niles Avenue, Suite D
St. Joseph, MI 49085

Website:
50andForward.com (coming in 2008)

Book orders may also be placed at
www.Amazon.com

50&Forward®
Devoted to the Journey Ahead®

About the Author

Jenna Mitchell Everett, CFP® is the founder and CEO of **50&Forward**® and an Associate Financial Advisor with the practice of Jim Everett, CFP®, Everett & Associates, a financial advisory practice of Ameriprise Financial Services, Inc.

For nearly 20 years Jenna has enjoyed educating her clients to make wise life and financial choices. Her passion for developing exceptional client relationships earned her Silver, Gold and Platinum Team Advisor awards from Amerprise Financial. Jenna was also selected by Ameriprise to provide national training in two areas: designing and implementing professional business plans and using interpersonal communications to improve client/advisor relationships.

Jenna's passion for educating and empowering women to make good financial and life choices makes her a sought after speaker by both corporations and non-profit organizations. Her most recent business venture is the founding of **50&Forward**®, a company providing services and products for the **50&Forward**® woman.

Jenna lives in St. Joseph, Michigan with her husband, Jim, and three sons.

Portrait by Meister-Witkowski Photography
Stevensville, Michigan

1008321

Made in the USA